FREIGHT ON STREET TRAMWAYS IN THE BRITISH ISLES

BY
DAVID VOICE

PUBLISHED BY ADAM GORDON

ALSO BY DAVID VOICE

How to Go Tram and Tramway Modelling
London's Tramways and How to Model Them
What Colour was that Tram?
Tramway Modelling in 'OO' Gauge
More Tramway Modelling in 'OO' Gauge
The Illustrated History of Kidderminster and Stourport Electric Tramway Company (with Melvyn Thompson)
How to Go Tram and Tramway Modelling, 2nd edition
The Millennium Guide to Trams in the British Isles
The Definitive Guide to Trams in the British Isles, 2nd edition
The Definitive Guide to Trams in the British Isles, 3rd edition
Toy and Model Trams of the World, Volume 1: Toys, Die-casts and Souvenirs (with Gottfried Kuře)
Toy and Model Trams of the World, Volume 2: Plastic, White Metal and Brass (with Gottfried Kuře)
Next Stop Seaton! (with David Jay)
How to Go Tram and Tramway Modelling, 3rd edition
Hospital Tramways and Railways, 1st and 2nd editions

Front Cover:
The parcel looks almost as big as the girl hoping to get it on to the Manchester tram, though it looks too large to get between the handrails and on to the platform. The object between the two ladies on the extreme left is either another package for the tramcar or may be a handcart the girl used to bring the large parcel to the tram stop.

Back Cover:
Top to bottom right:
1) Very mixed freight on the Dublin Tramways.
2) Chesterfield tramcar towing a goods wagon. The notices in the windows say "Engaged for J.W. Simpson". So it is on private hire and presumably the goods wagon is carrying items for the event. It looks like a water boiler. Note the notice on the dash "TRAILER BEHIND".
3) The Alford and Sutton Tramway handled all kinds of freight, mainly in open wagons as shown on this mixed train of goods and passenger vehicles.
4) Lots of activity on the Wisbech and Upwell Tramway as perishable fruit is loaded on to goods vans.

Tickets:
Top: Manchester Corporation Tramways had attractive pre-paid tickets (based very much on post office stamps) for their parcels service.
Bottom: Parcel ticket from the Glasgow Tramway and Omnibus Company, a horse tramway that operated from 1872 to 1896.

© David Voice 2007

All rights reserved. No part of this publication may be reproduced, stored in a retrieval system or transmitted in any form or by any means electronic, mechanical, photocopying, recording or otherwise, without prior permission in writing from the author David Voice.
British Library Cataloguing in Publication Data
Voice, David

ISBN 978-1-874422-66-2
Publication no. 70
Printing limited to 300 copies
2nd printing limited to 150 copies
3rd printing (2008) limited to 150 copies

Published in 2007 by Adam Gordon, Kintradwell Farm, Brora, Sutherland KW9 6LU
Tel: 01408 622660
E-mail: adam@ahg-books.com
Printed by 4edge Ltd, Hockley, Essex SS5 4AD
Production by trevor@epic.gb.com

CONTENTS

Introduction		5
Part 1	Parcels Services	11
Part 2	Postal Services	21
Part 3	Farming and Livestock	27
Part 4	Mineral Traffic	33
Part 5	Road-Rail Services	41
Part 6	Other Goods	43
Part 7	Internal Freight	55
Appendices	Tramway Systems that Operated a Parcels Service	62
	Tramway Systems that Operated a Postal Service	62
Acknowledgements and Sources		63

Where it all started, on 30 August 1860 in Birkenhead. George Train is on the far left of the top deck with his arm outstretched.

The complete fleet in Kidderminster, none looking suitable for carrying animals or coal. In fact they only ever carried parcels.

INTRODUCTION

From the very beginnings in 1860 when an American, George Train, opened his horse drawn tramway in Birkenhead, street tramways in the British Isles have been associated with passenger transport. However, even in those early days, the builders and operators were ready to take on any enterprise that would increase receipts and hence profit. At this time it was not clear what the legal situation was. George Train built his London horse tramway in 1861 with the agreement of the local parish vestry. But they all found themselves in court and found guilty of a public nuisance and George Train had to remove the rails. The only legal way to put tracks in the street was to have a private Act of Parliament allowing the tramway to be built and run. This was a very expensive and lengthy process. As it became evident that tramway systems were a beneficial transport for cities and towns there was pressure to simplify the legal process. This led to passing of the Tramways Act 1870, which enabled tramways to be built after the passing of a Provisional Order. The Act contains a paragraph stating "Every such Provisional Order shall specify the nature of the traffic for which such tramway is to be used, and the tolls and charges which may be demanded and taken by the promoters in respect of the same, and shall contain such regulations relating to such traffic and such tolls and charges as the Board of Trade shall deem necessary and proper."

A sample Provisional Order was soon made available to prospective tramway promoters and in the nature of such things it contained catch-all clauses. A good example is the 1896 Bill resulting from the Provisional Order passed for the Kidderminster and Stourport Electric Tramway which contains the following paragraphs:

52 The Company may demand and take in respect of any animals, goods, materials, articles, or things conveyed by them on the Tramways, including every expense incidental to the conveyance any rates or charges, not exceeding the following:

ANIMALS

For every horse, mule, or other beast of draught or burden, fourpence per head per mile;

For every ox, cow, bull, or head of cattle, threepence per head per mile;

For calves, pigs, sheep, and small animals, one penny per head per mile.

It is hard to imagine this pristine tramway with its sparkling trams and top-hatted guests might well have had to carry London's sewage on its system.

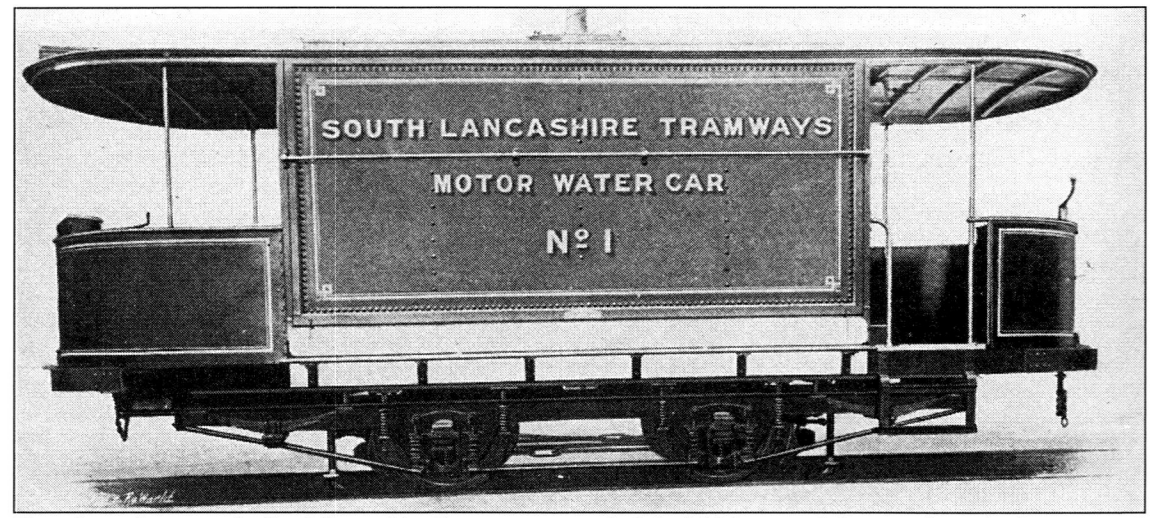

The only works car on the South Lancashire Tramways system, had the initial proposals for a goods service been accepted there would have been a whole fleet of works cars.

GOODS

For all coals, coke, culm [coal dust], charcoal, cannel [a type of coal], limestone, chalk, lime, salt, sand, fireclay, cinders, dung, compost, and all sorts of manure, and all undressed materials for the repair of public roads or highways, twopence per ton per mile;

For all iron, ironstone, iron ore, pig iron, bar iron, rod iron, sheet iron, hoop iron, plates of iron, slabs, billets and rolled iron, bricks, slag, and stone, stones for building, pitching, and paving, tiles slates, and clay (except fireclay), and for wrought iron not otherwise specially classed herein, and for heavy iron castings, including railway chairs, twopence halfpenny per ton per mile;

For all sugar, grain, corn, flour, hides, dyewoods, earthenware, timber, staves, deals, and metals (except iron), nails, anvils, vices, and chains, and for light iron castings, threepence per ton per mile;

For cotton, wools, drugs, manufactured goods, and all other wares, merchandise, fish, articles, matters, or things not otherwise specially classed herein, fourpence per ton per mile.

SMALL PACKAGES

For any parcel not exceeding seven pounds in weight, threepence;

For any parcel exceeding seven pounds and not exceeding fourteen pounds in weight, fivepence;

For any parcel exceeding fourteen pounds and not exceeding twenty-eight pounds in weight, sevenpence;

For any parcel exceeding twenty-eight pounds and not exceeding fifty-six pounds in weight, ninepence;

For any parcel exceeding fifty-six pounds and not exceeding five hundred pounds in weight, such sum as the Company may think fit;

Provided always, that articles sent in large aggregate quantities, although made up in separate parcels, such as bags of sugar, coffee, meal, and the like, shall not be deemed small parcels, but that term shall apply only to single parcels in separate packages.

FOR THE CARRIAGE OF SINGLE ARTICLES OF GREAT WEIGHT

For the carriage of any iron boiler, cylinder, or single piece of machinery, or single piece of timber or stone, or other single article, the weight of which, including the carriage, shall exceed four tons, but shall not exceed eight tons, such sum as the Company may think fit, not exceeding two shillings per ton per mile;

For the carriage of any single piece of timber, stone, machinery, or other single article, the weight of which, with the carriage, shall exceed eight tons, such sum as the Company may feel fit.

REGULATIONS AS TO RATES

For articles or animals conveyed on the tramways for a less distance than two miles, the Company may demand rates and charges as for two miles;

For the fraction of a ton the Company may demand rates according to the number of quarters of a ton in such fraction shall be deemed a quarter of a ton;

With respect to all articles except stone and timber, the weight shall be determined according to the usual avoirdupois weight;

With respect to stone and timber, fourteen cubic feet of stone, forty cubic feet of oak, mahogany, teak, beech, or ash, and fifty cubic feet of any other timber, shall be deemed one ton weight, and so in proportion for any smaller quantity.

53 The Company shall not be bound, unless they think fit, to carry passengers' luggage exceeding the weight in this Act in that behalf mentioned, nor any parcel or goods.

54 No goods, animals, articles or things other than passengers and passengers' luggage and parcels not exceeding fifty-six pounds in weight, shall be conveyed on the Tramways between the hours of eight in the morning and eight in the evening without the consent of the local authority and the road authority, nor shall any carriages, trucks, or wagons, constructed for use upon a railroad be permitted to pass along the Tramways between the same hours without such consent.

Despite having all these powers the tramway only ever offered a modest parcels service. Indeed it never had any rolling stock that could carry most of the materials listed. The fleet always consisted of ordinary passenger tramcars. However, it does demonstrate that promoters would want to cover every possibility, just in case their tramway had the opportunity to carry freight.

A more unusual example of moving freight has been found in the Acts empowering the London United Tramways Company and the Metropolitan Electric Tramways Company to build their lines in the London suburbs. It was common for the local councils in which tram routes were sought to seek to profit from the proposals. They often insisted on onerous requirements, particularly regarding the widening of roads and relaying road surfaces at the cost of the tramway company. However some of the London local councils went even further. They had written into the Acts:

(7) The council may with their own carriages or trucks at any time between the hours of twelve at night and six in the morning use all or any of the said tramways free of toll for sanitary purposes and for the conveyance of scavenging refuse, road material and nightsoil and the council may make such junctions sidings and works as they may think necessary or convenient for making connection to the said tramways from their depots and yards or sewage farm. Provided that the council

This Chesterfield tramcar is towing a goods wagon. The notices in the windows say "Engaged for J.W. Simpson". So it is on private hire and presumably the goods wagon is carrying items for the event. It looks like a water boiler. Note the notice on the dash "TRAILER BEHIND".

A Dublin and Lucan goods tramcar designed to carry all kinds of items in large quantities.

shall not under or by virtue of this section acquire any right to convey scavenging refuse or night-soil on any of the said tramways within the district of any other district council without the consent of other such council but such consent shall not be withheld if upon application of either the Company or the council the Board of Trade shall after enquiry be of opinion that the consent should be given subject to the insertion therein of such terms and conditions for the protection of such council as to the Board of Trade shall seem reasonable. The council may themselves provide and use horse power upon the said tramways for the purposes of this section or if they so require the Company shall supply them at a reasonable charge with electric or other motive power for the purposes aforesaid the council at their own expense providing carriages or trucks suitable to be used on the said tramways with the motive power for the time being used by the company.

Not all the local councils had these provisions written into the Act, but over half the councils involved did insist on such provisions. Again in reality none actually used these powers and so Londoners were spared the sight (or more likely sound and smell) of sewage trams travelling along the roads in the dead of night taking their unpleasant loads for disposal.

There was a similar thought in Chesterfield where the Council ordered a report in 1908 on the practicality of transporting night-soil along the tram tracks at night, it is presumed in trailers towed by tramcars. However the Tramway Manager and the "Inspector of Nuisances" both objected to the proposal and it was quietly forgotten.

In 1901 a leading member of the Tramways and Light Railways Association, Alfred H. Gibbings, addressed the British Association to advocate the use of tramways for

The LCC took advantage of some of its goods trams to advertise its services.

Two freight trams pass on the Camborne and Redruth Tramway in Cornwall.

the carriage of freight and in particular he focussed on the freight potential of the South Lancashire systems. He repeated this to the Liverpool Engineering Society in 1902. His idea was to have tram and trailer sets taking freight to and from the docks and distributing goods to either private sidings on commercial premises or centrally located goods depots. The trams and trailers would be based on similar service operated on American interurban lines; that is, bogie enclosed vans providing an Express service.

What these examples do show is that in the late 1800s and early 1900s people had no clear understanding of the role or impact of tramways upon their communities. This is not surprising as, until the arrival of the electric tram, movement on British streets was confined to walking, horses or on rare occasions a steam traction engine. By far the majority of the people had no option other than to

One of the two Dresden CarGo trams used to take automobile parts to and from the Volkswagen factory in the city.

walk; the very rich had their horse carriages, but for most the only horse drawn vehicles they experienced were carts, usually moving goods around. Horses were limited in power and particularly when going uphill. Traction engines were very powerful but extremely

In Zurich the tram set is parked in the suburbs for local people to take their unwanted goods for recycling.

slow and used mainly to transport very large or heavy items. So when the electric tram arrived many were truly amazed. Even the early small tramcars were far bigger than any horse cart or carriage. They could carry what was an unbelievable number of passengers, they appeared to have no visible form of power and they would glide, apparently effortlessly, up steep gradients. It must have seemed to an observer of the day that the tram was capable of doing anything. However, the tramway operators soon realised that although the tramcar could undertake all kinds of tasks, it could only do so along its prescribed routes. In many instances this proved viable and profitable for the tramway. In 1915 the General Managers of Salford and Bury tramways combined to present a paper on "Utilisation of Tramways for Goods Traffic" where they reviewed the then current situation regarding the use of tramways to carry goods traffic and concluded that there was potential for much more use of tramways in this respect, particularly supplying raw materials to factories. They suggested that such operation was not only viable but also profitable and that adjoining tramways should cooperate more to interchange goods traffic. There was a discussion after the presentation and it is clear that there was significant reluctance by other tramway General Managers in identifying the profitability of such goods traffic. In fact little, if any, additional goods traffic appeared on tramways as a result of the talk. The vast majority of goods carried by tramways was confined to parcels or similar sized items.

Today in the British Isles only the Manx Electric Railway offers any freight service. All the newly constructed tramways are strictly passengers only. However, this may not always be so. On the continent there are some instances of freight services being introduced. In Dresden two new purpose built tramcars (CarGo Trams) were introduced in 2001 to transport car parts to and from the Volkswagen factory in the city. While in Zurich there are two special services, introduced in 2003. The tramway operates a special freight tram and two trailers with a scheduled timetable for the collection of bulky items for disposal to recycling and separately a similar service for redundant electrical goods. It is always possible that the new British tramways might introduce their own freight services.

A most unusual load – a Blackpool and Fleetwood Tramroad crossbench car hauls a redundant Lancashire boiler from Bispham depot to Rigby Road, for disposal. See Chapter 6.

Part 1
PARCELS SERVICES

From the earliest days the tramways companies were constantly looking for ways of increasing their revenue. Parcels services began in the horse tramway days, while in Accrington the local steam tramway offered the service. Conductors carried tickets (actually they were more like stamps that were stuck onto the parcel to show a fee had been paid) and were authorised to accept parcels up to 56 pounds in weight for delivery along the route or within half a mile of the tramway receiving offices. For example in Liverpool the Liverpool Tramways and Omnibus Company, a horse tramway, was authorised to carry parcels, other than passengers' luggage. In 1888 the charges were set at:

Not exceeding 7lb	3d any distance
Between 7 and 14lb	5d any distance
Between 14 and 28lb	7d any distance
Between 28 and 56lb	9d any distance
Over 56lb	What the company thinks fit

The parcels were carried on the driver's platform and it was up to the customer to arrange delivery to and collection from identified points on the tramway system. It is unlikely that the parcels service provided a significant sum for the company.

When electricity was introduced tramway systems grew far larger and travel was much faster. No doubt in the early days the electric systems continued to allow passengers to take parcels with them at a charge, just as dogs were charged as an addition to the passenger fare. From this point it seems that the approach now varied according to whether the system was operated by the Council or by a private company. Councils were very clear in the way they saw their responsibilities in regard to tramways. With some exceptions they saw tramways as being for the convenience of the public and should offer an economical and effective means of carrying passengers from one point to another. They did not see themselves setting up in competition to the Post Office. So up to the First World War very few Council tramways offered a parcels service (Manchester being one of the exceptions). The private companies had different responsibilities. They had to

It is difficult for us to realise just how busy the streets were in the horse tramway days. This is Liverpool and it demonstrates how useful a parcels service would have been for the traders and the people of the city.

give the best return possible to their shareholders. So any additional means of income were used. So most offered a full parcels service. The first comprehensive parcels service appears to have been established by the Potteries Tramways in Stoke on Trent. This was a success, and twice a day the tramway would attach a trailer to the service cars to carry heavier items. By 1906 the tramway had one goods car, six parcels trailers (numbers 109-114); three motorised coal trams (numbers 106, 108 and 118) and one motorised tipper wagon (number 124). The BET took the principle to their Birmingham and Black Country Tramways and instituted a parcels service. The idea of a parcels service then seems to have been taken onto all BET tramway systems. In Birmingham the Corporation had been acquiring the company tramways. To begin with the BET continued its parcels service in the city with the cooperation of the Corporation. But around 1908 the Corporation leased the parcels rights to Messrs Cain and Cartwright. The parcels were carried on the trams by messengers. However, the venture was not a success and Birmingham Corporation ceased a parcels service and only carried newspapers.

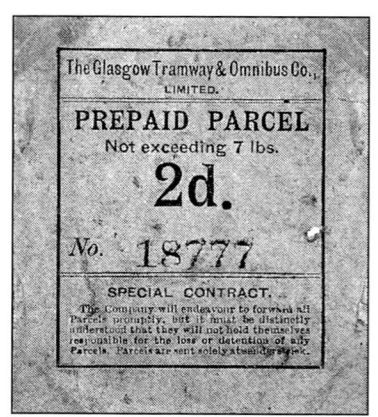

Parcel ticket from the Glasgow Tramway and Omnibus Company, a horse tramway that operated from 1872 to 1896.

In Accrington the steam tramway offered a parcels service.

In the Black Country a very successful parcels service was operated with dedicated motor trams and wagons. Here parcels car 6 hauls an open wagon full of large boxes.

A good example of a small system offering a parcels service is Kidderminster. Basically a one route service the system went from the east of Kidderminster, through the town centre and on through farmland to Stourport on Severn. It offered a Tramway Parcels Express (TPE) service. In addition to the tramway offices in the centre of the town, the company also had arrangements with a hairdresser, umbrella shop and newsagent in Kidderminster and a printers and stationers in Stourport. The tramway offered to collect and deliver parcels within a half mile distance of the tram route. The charges ranged from 2d for a parcel weighing up to 7lb to 6d for a massive 56lb parcel. It is assumed that a lad with a barrow would do the collection and delivery away from the route while the tramcars would carry the parcels for most of the distance. The tramway company were at pains to show that their service was considerably cheaper than the railway parcels service and the Post Office parcel post. The demands on parcels express services could not have been great as all the parcels were carried by the ordinary passenger trams as part of their scheduled service. Indeed the tramway never owned any goods trailers or works trams.

The nearby Black Country Tramways, owned by the same company, was able to offer a far

Transferring parcels from the horse drawn van to the tramcar on the Black Country Tramway.

Manchester was another tramway with dedicated parcels tramcars and a very profitable parcels operation.

An indication of the volume and variety of traffic handled by the Parcels Department in Manchester.

Lots of parcels arriving in the main sorting office of the Manchester Tramways Parcel Service.

larger service. With through running agreements with Birmingham, Black Country trams were able to offer the service over a considerable area. The service started around the turn of the century and its favourable rates soon saw a significant growth in its business. So soon after 1910 special "Parcels Express" vans were added by rebuilding some four passenger cars. These were stripped of all seats and the sides boarded in to enable the maximum number of parcels to be carried. Like the smaller Kidderminster tramway, the system used both its own offices and commissioned agents to act as collecting shops, though again parcels would be collected and delivered off the tramway routes by lads with hand carts. Just before the First World War the service expanded again with the tramway linking with Midland Red motor buses to allow distribution into country areas. The service was renamed "Tramway Parcels and Motor Express". One or more open wagon trailers were also added to the parcels fleet to increase the carrying capacity. The service further prospered when companies found that they could send goods in bulk by rail to Birmingham. Then the loads were split and taken by tram and bus to their destinations throughout the Black Country. This could save several days, due to the time it took the railways to trans-ship goods and take them to local stations. Such was the demand for this service that the tramway company built a warehouse in Smethwick with a special spur to store and trans-ship goods coming by rail.

On the Blackpool to Fleetwood tramroad a member of the public and his son are about to give a parcel to the tram driver. They appear to have used the family pram to carry the parcel to the tramway.

Other tramways with their own special parcels vans included Manchester. Such was the Manchester service that they guaranteed delivery of parcels the same day anywhere in the city, provided the parcel was brought to them by 3.45pm. A particular feature of the Manchester service was that, using pre-paid tramway parcel stamps, a parcel could be handed to the conductor of any tramcar. He would then hand it over at the next parcels office. Indeed shoppers could choose their purchases in the city stores in the morning, have them delivered in the afternoon and pay cash on delivery! To provide the service seven special parcels cars were used. There was a slight problem for Manchester tramways – the system had a through running agreement with the Ashton-Under-Lyne Corporation tramway for its passenger cars. But it also sent its parcels car onto Ashton rails. They were told to cease as the van ran without paying for the electricity it consumed from the Ashton overhead wire.

A posed publicity photograph of a customer handing over a parcel on the Manchester tramway system.

In Blackburn a parcels boy waits for the next tram with a parcel ready on his sack truck. The parcel will be handed to the driver and the boy will be off to collect his next parcel.

Again in Blackburn a parcels boy walks back to the parcels office and waiting room having handed a parcel to the driver.

In Blackburn the parcels service began in 1907 with just two parcels boys. It proved very popular and became a valuable income generator. By 1914 the tramway employed 42 parcels boys, indicating how much the service had expanded. Indeed in Blackburn and many other systems it was a good way for young lads to become employees of the tramway. Starting as a parcels boy they could be recognised as a diligent worker and move to other roles in the tramway, possibly eventually becoming drivers or inspectors. The life of the parcels boy was not without its hazards. In 1915 a Blackburn parcels boy mistimed his jump onto a moving tram and fell to the road receiving heavy bruising to his face. In the days without sick pay he would

In Blackburn, obviously there is no parcels boy around, as the conductor has had to take the parcel to the parcels office himself.

have regretted his error in both pain and pocket.

Nearby in Burnley they experimented in 1912 with a wagon trailer to carry heavy parcels, those from 56lb to 5cwt. The wagon was propelled by service tramcars and ran at specific times. At the terminus it would wait the usual ten minutes with its service car and the people or companies using the service would have to time their collection to be there as the wagon arrived. However, this aspect of the parcels service did not gain the popularity that was hoped and the regular service ceased after a couple of years. However, the wagon would be used if there was a demand for sufficient goods to be moved around the tramway system. The most fascinating aspect of this service was that the wagon was not towed by the tramcars, but was placed in front of the service tramcar and pushed. The argument was that by having the wagon in front of the tram the driver always had it in sight, if it was being towed at the back it would be under the control of the conductor, who would only be able to attend to it when they were not collecting fares. So the argument was that pushing the wagon was safer and more convenient.

With the coming of the First World War it was realised by the government that the tramways could ease the pressure on road goods carriage by taking

Cheltenham Tramway's parcel service used motor vehicles to deliver parcels around the town.

Cheltenham also had less state of the art transport in the form of bicycles. The extent of the parcels service can be gauged from the number of parcels boys employed.

17

Transferring parcels from a hand cart to the goods van on the Clogher Valley tramway at Augher.

parcels and so they asked all the tramway undertakings to help in this way. This meant that those Councils who had rejected the idea of offering a parcels service had to reconsider their position. In some instances the necessary preparations took a while. In Leeds it was not until April 1918 that the parcels service came into operation. Not an enormous help to the War effort. Stores car number 1 was converted to parcels service. However, the service was a success and the operation extended in cooperation with the Bradford and Halifax tramway systems. By 1919 some 30 boys were employed to collect and deliver parcels to points up to half a mile from the tram routes. Bradford introduced two trolleybus lorries specifically for their service.

One difficulty of the joint services was that each of the tramways had different gauges. So the goods had to be offloaded at the boundary and reloaded to the next system. This multiple handling led to extra costs and a natural move to find ways of eliminating the extra handling. So motor vans were purchased and later some buses were converted to vans. By the mid 1920s there were four motor vans and 60 staff. By now the vans had taken on most of the carriage work and the parcels tram was no longer needed and it reverted back to its former role as an ordinary stores van and the involvement of trams in the service finished.

On the Isle of Man the Manx Electric Railway had a virtual monopoly for the parcels service along the whole of the east coast and most of the north of the island. In the early days horse carts were based at Douglas and Ramsey for distribution away from the line. Later motor-lorries and vans replaced the horses. The service was very popular and from the 1920s to the 1960s the parcel and freight services accounted for 10% of the traffic on the tramway. However, the demand for the service declined as road competition increased. So the full parcels service ceased in 1966, though items continued to be carried from station to station.

Perhaps the most unusual reason for developing a parcels service must be Brighton Corporation. In 1914 the Corporation introduced a new service for the public. Those

Seen in the window of an antiques shop is this sign identifying a parcels office that was on the Bath Tramways system. Unfortunately the shop was closed and this is the best photograph that could be taken.

This parcels hand cart has been preserved and is on display at the Manchester Museum of Transport. It was used to take parcels to and from the tramway.

who had borrowed books from the town's libraries could return the books by handing them and a fee of 1p to the conductor of a passing tramcar. This proved popular and soon other items could be sent by tram and so the parcels service began. It continued until 1920, by which time competition from other carriers meant that demand for the service dropped to an uneconomic level. With a similar locally orientated provision, the Huddersfield tramway offered a service where wives could send freshly cooked dinner, in its can, by tramcar to their husband's factory and all for 3d per six-day week.

One of the most successful tramways parcels service was that run by the Dublin United Tramways Company. The parcels service, like so many, began in a small way. In this instance it was in 1883 that a service was opened for the Rathmines area using the horse trams. This grew into a very successful and profitable service. By 1897 the parcels service was given its own five pages in the DUTC timetable. The service thrived and in 1908 the company had to introduce a new rule to counter an initiative by enterprising individuals. They would provide a competing parcels services by carrying parcels and using the tramway to deliver them. They were taking advantage of the rule that a passenger's personal luggage would go free provided it weighed less than 28lb. The tramway company felt that this was in direct competition to their parcels service, so the new rule defined workmen's tools, hawkers' baskets, bundles of washing, messengers' packages and all parcels as not personal luggage. So a fee of 2d per item was charged. It was anticipated that this would increase income by a thousand pounds a year. Between 1909 and 1924 the service expanded to include all kinds of other goods. These are covered in the following chapters. The parcels service was interrupted in 1916 by the Easter rising. Some of the tramway infrastructure and at least one tram were damaged. But the company did its best to reintroduce its services including the parcels service to assist businesses to get back to normality. In 1919 the parcels service was picked out for praise by the Tramway and Railway World. This reported that the DUTC had a system of vans and messengers to distribute to destinations away from the tram routes. The company also managed the whole of the parcels traffic for the Dublin and South Eastern Railway Company as well as delivering all the Dublin bound parcels for the London and North Western Railway Company. Income from the parcels traffic was £9,178 per annum and covered an area from Howth in the north-east to Dalkey in the south-east. The parcels service closed in

1940 due to a combination of tram route closures and replacement by buses and the inevitable competition from other road carriers.

It seems from our perspective that the tramway was increasing its revenue by requiring conductors and drivers to take on extra work, probably without additional pay. The pressure was even greater when it is realised that conductors were often under threat of dismissal if they missed the delivery of a parcel. However, there were some compensations. For example in Brighton it is recorded that the fishmonger would send a package of fish at the end of the week for the driver and conductor delivering his fish. Brighton tramway employees were banned from entering Public Houses in uniform, except one, the Globe at Newton. This was because it was a parcels office and it was known that tramway employees would make up 'false' parcels in order to enter the pub.

Not all parcels services were as successful as Dublin. The Ipswich Corporation Tramway started its parcel service in 1904. It was met with considerable indifference and was little used. So the service was discontinued in 1906 having had a life of less than two years. Even shorter was the experiment with a parcels service by Pontypridd Urban District Council lasting a mere six months in 1914.

Over the last few years new tramway systems have been built in British cities. All of these have focussed entirely on passenger services and none offer any parcels service. When I was travelling on the Croydon Tramlink I saw a passenger who entered carrying a large boxed television set which was put in the space for wheelchair users. Similarly I have seen bicycle users taking their bikes onto trams. It seems that some passengers have found the carrying capacity of the trams very useful and they take objects that would be impossible to load onto buses.

The narrow gauge heritage tramway in Seaton does not advertise a parcels service, but I believe that it has on occasions carried goods by special arrangement. However there is one tramway in the British Isles that continues to offer a public parcels service. This is the Manx Electric Railway. Indeed the system has several goods van trailers that are used for parcels work. I had direct experience on one occasion when at the Douglas terminal of the tramway. The tram I was about to travel on had a goods van attached behind the passenger trailer. A pick up truck arrived and the crew transferred a barrel of beer from the truck to the van. On arrival at Ramsey the barrel was unloaded ready for delivery to a pub or hotel. Other than the barrel the van itself was empty. Once emptied the van was detached from the tram and trailer and gravity shunted to a spur siding, I presume to wait for the exchange empty barrel that would be taken back behind another scheduled passenger service.

A list of all the systems that have offered parcels services at some stage in their existence is given in Appendix 1.

The Southmet operated a parcels service for a short period. Note the "T.P.E." on the wicker baskets standing for "Tramway Parcels Express", while the canvass sack is marked with the tramway initials "S.M.E.T.".

A parcels stamp used by Brighton Tramways.

Part 2
POSTAL SERVICES

The Postmaster General had the powers to compel any tramway to carry mail. However, in practice such arrangements were the subject of agreements between the tramways and the General Post Office. Tramways provided two types of service to the postal authorities and the public. The first was carrying bulk mail. That is moving sacks of mail from one sorting office to another. The railways did a great deal of such work, indeed there was sufficient mail carried that there were special trains, including the renowned mobile sorting offices, where letters were sorted en route from one city to another. However bulk transport of mail was rare on passenger tramways. There is only one tramway that had a wagon identified to carry mail. This is the Manx Electric Railway where enclosed wagon number 4 was painted red and carried the Royal Mail name and the royal ER logo for the 1993 centenary celebrations. This wagon carried mail sacks and was also used to take first day commemorative envelopes with Manx stamps picturing the MER. The GPO mail contract was won by the Manx Electric Railway in 1879, but it was cancelled and then renewed in 1903. Sacks were carried between the sorting offices at Douglas and Ramsey. The mail sacks were taken to the tramcars by Royal Mail vans. Along the route there were post boxes by various tram stops and these were emptied by conductors and carried to the terminus and handed over to the GPO. In order that this could be done the conductors were sworn in as auxiliary postmen. They were then allowed

On the Manx Electric Railway mail bags are transferred from the tramway to the GPO van.

The Manx Electric Railway repainted van number 4 in Post Office red with the royal cipher, showing that the MER carried mail for the Post Office.

to empty post boxes and handle letters. The contract continued until 1972 when the line was only operated during the summer season. Later the policy was changed and the line opened throughout the year. It is understood that the contract was renewed for transporting bulk mail.

Other tramways that carried mail sacks did so either on the driver's platform of normal service passenger trams or in works cars usually used for tramway operation purposes. A GPO employee would load the sacks onto the tramcar and a similar employee would unload the sacks at their destination.

The second and more common service was the provision of postal letter boxes fixed to specific tramcar services. The box had to be securely fixed in place and sometimes this was as crude as chaining it to the handbrake with a padlock. The first tramway to carry GPO letter boxes on its trams was Huddersfield in 1887 which fixed postal boxes onto its steam tram trailers. The system was unusual in carrying the boxes all day with hourly collections. At this time it was possible to hail a tram to stop at any point on its route. However, if the stop was only for the purpose of posting a letter the conductor

Mail sacks being loaded onto the Manx Electric goods van at Ramsey to be taken to Douglas by the tramway.

Blackpool's Railcoach number 633 when it was used as the world's only Post Office Tram. There was a counter selling stamps and postcards inside the tramcar.

Huddersfield with the tram on the right carrying a post box on the dash. The tram on the left might have a similar box but they were mounted at the rear of the tramcar and this view shows the front of the tramcar.

would charge an additional 1d that was taken as part of the fare collection. The postal boxes continued to be fitted to trams after the system was electrified in 1901 though the extra 1d charge was dropped. Every tramcar had a postal box attached to the rear dash panel and they were now emptied every two hours by GPO officials. The postal box service continued until 1939, a year prior to the closure of the tramway, although in latter years the post boxes were only fitted to a few trams and a couple of replacement trolleybuses.

An interesting case of the introduction of postal boxes was seen on the Blackpool and Fleetwood Tramroad Company. In 1902 the residents of Cleveleys had become frustrated with the poor postal service they were getting. It was suggested that the tramroad should place postal boxes at the tramroad stations and on their trams. This service commenced in 1903 with a post box carried hourly. The postal cars were met by a GPO official at Talbot Road, who transported the letters to Blackpool Post Office. By 1908 the Post Office had introduced the more normal procedure of collecting mail from the post boxes at the tramroad stations using their own mail vans. So the tramroad ceased to carry post boxes on the tramcars. However, for a while the tramroad station masters continued to be responsible for emptying their post boxes at the end of the day and handing the mail bags to the next tramcar to take to Blackpool. This appears to be the last such service offered by Blackpool until 1981 when car 627 was given Post Office posters and had a post box fitted inside. This was successful and in 1982 tramcar 633 was chosen as an all over advertisement for the GPO services. In addition six seats were removed from the interior to allow a post office counter to be set up and stamps and other postal material were sold in the tram during normal post office hours. Passengers could also use a post box in the tramcar to post letters and postcards. This service continued through the 1983 season, but proved uneconomic and in 1984 the counter was removed, the seats replaced and a stamp machine placed by the post box. The contract for the advertising finished in 1985 and the tram was repainted in a different advertisement and the post box and stamp machine were removed. While it ran it was advertised as the World's first and only Post Office Tram.

In other towns and cities the provision of a post box on trams tended to come much later. It was only after the First World War that the idea really caught on in the

Another posed publicity photograph showing mail being posted in one of the post boxes carried on a Huddersfield tramcar.

In Manchester another posed photograph shows the mail being handed to a Post Office official by the conductor. Note the "POST CAR" stencil just under the destination box on the front of the tramcar.

23

Restored Manchester number 765 when on loan to Blackpool showing the "POST CAR" stencil above the destination box. In reality this was just for display, it did not have a post box when in Blackpool.

This unusual photograph shows the post box being taken off the tramcar in Camborne.

24

larger towns and cities. The boxes were carefully designed to ensure that they were securely fixed to the tramcar dash and could only be opened by GPO employees, who met the trams at pre-arranged points on the route. The boxes were usually carried on the trams late in the evening to allow mail that had missed the last collection from static boxes to get to the sorting office. On the railway mail trains there were late posting boxes, but letters had to carry a late posting fee and they received a special TPO (Travelling Post Office) franking. Letters posted in tramcar mobile post boxes were treated like ordinary mail, so had no extra charge and no special franking.

The late running of the postal trams meant that they were seldom photographed. The dark evenings were difficult conditions for photography, so those photos that are found are usually posed.

Finally in the Isle of Man there was a rather unusual example of postal use of trams. This concerned the Snaefell Mountain Railway. It is admitted that its link with street tramways is a little tenuous, but it is owned and run by the Manx Electric Railway that does have quite a few miles of roadside running. The railway (the only electric mountain railway in the British Isles) was built and opened in 1889. At the same time the Snaefell Summit Hotel was opened. This catered for tourists selling mainly souvenirs, meals and refreshments. To encourage sales of postcards the hotel made use of an idea previously used in other tourist areas.

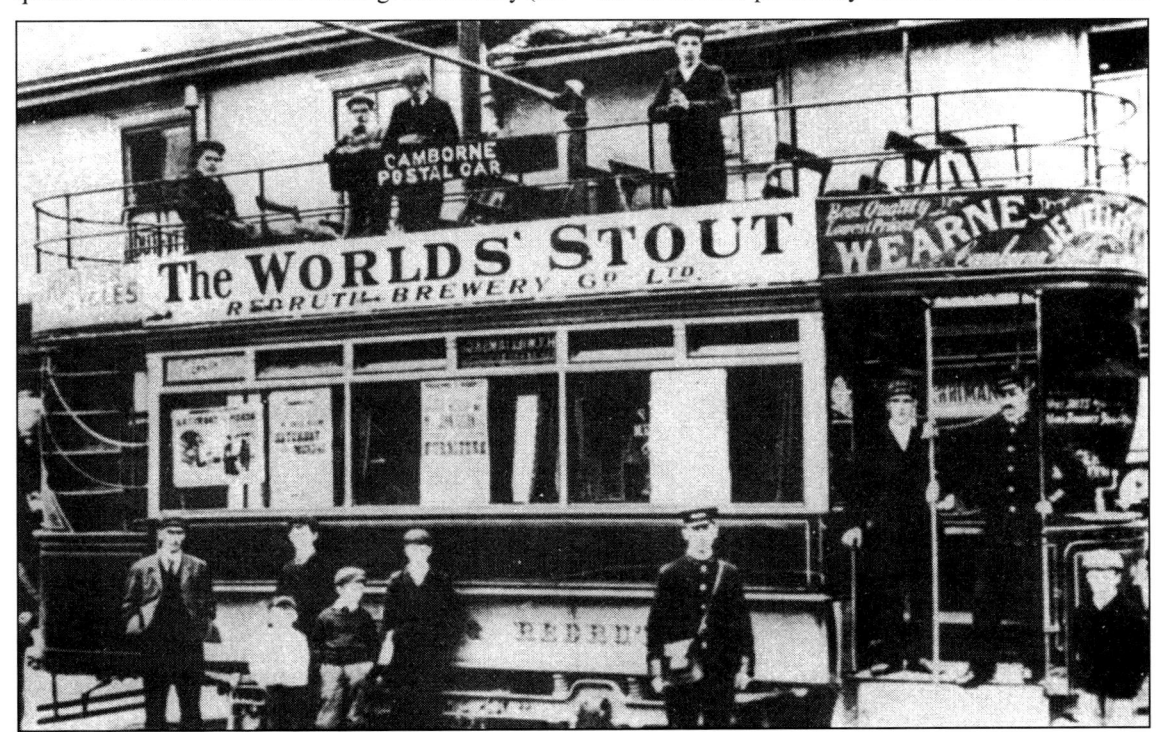

Camborne tramcar number 2 with a post box on the dash.

Again on the Camborne Tramway, this time with car number 1. The car carries a sign on the upper deck railings stating it is a Postal Car.

25

Again at Camborne with tramcar number 4 carrying a post box on the dash.

This was the practice of placing a local hand franking or cachet on the postcard to indicate that it had been purchased actually at the place indicated. So in 1904 the hotel would offer these cachets on postcards purchased and posted in the hotel. The cachet consisted of a diamond shaped hand stamp with the words "Snaefell Summit IOM" and the date. Tourists would purchase the postcard and appropriate postage and write their message and the address of the recipient on the card, then post the card in a post box in the hotel. What few realised was that the post box was a private posting box. Hotel staff would take the postcards and apply the cachet, then take the cards by mountain tram to Laxey and sometimes then by MER to Douglas and post them in a regular GPO post box, possibly in the post box at Laxey that was emptied by the MER conductors. Later the postcards could be purchased with the cachet already applied so they would not need to be posted at the summit, though most were. This service was run continuously, stopping only for wars or the occasion when the hotel burnt down.

A list of all the systems that offered GPO services at some stage in their existence is given in Appendix 2.

Tramways in other countries also carried the mail, as shown by this photo of a New York, Third Avenue, tram mail cable car.

Part 3
FARMING AND LIVESTOCK

Street tramways are always associated with towns and cities, with inner city travel and urban commuting. So it comes as a surprise to find that several systems offered specific services for farmers and market gardeners. Some are fairly obvious. That street tramway that is on the edge of the definition, the Wisbech and Upwell Tramway, has many railway characteristics (not least of which was being owned by British Railways). It ran alongside a road from Cambridgeshire to Norfolk, in a strong farming area.

In today's towns and cities the idea of buses carrying farm produce and even animals seems absurd. But in the early part of the 20th century the conurbations were not so large and the outer termini of the tramway systems were often very rural. An example of the mixed nature of tramways is the small system linking

On the Wisbech and Upwell Tramway the extensive sidings at Upwell crowded with vans shows how busy the tramway was carrying farm produce from the rich growing area of the Fenlands to their markets in London and other cities.

A seemingly endless line of goods vans carry the farm produce from Upwell to Wisbech along the quiet Norfolk roads. Motorists not used to the area must have got quite a shock when they came across this.

The Wisbech and Upwell Tramway did not just haul goods vans, here a line of mostly open wagons go along the road near Elm Bridge.

Kidderminster with Stourport. Though having only a few miles on basically one route the tramway travelled through farming country. In the 1920s the company asked the Board of Trade for permission to raise its fares. The response was to ask why there were fares given for journeys within Kidderminster and within Stourport and a fare for journeys from one town to the other, but no fares for stops between the towns. The answer from the company was that there was only farm land between the towns and there were no stops on that part of the route.

So it is after all not so surprising that some tramway operators sought to increase revenue from the carriage of produce and even animals. Tramways even had rates of fares for small poultry. This raises images of the Harold Lloyd film where he wins a live turkey on Christmas Eve and his adventures trying to get it home in a crowded streetcar. But in reality only two systems allowed unaccompanied livestock. These were Dublin and Halifax, and then the livestock had to be crated.

More understandable was the transport of milk churns. Full churns would be taken by early morning

Lots of activity on the Wisbech and Upwell Tramway as perishable fruit is loaded onto goods vans.

28

Another roadside running steam tram, the Wantage Tramway, also carried farm produce.

More farm traffic on the Wantage Tramway.

The Manx Electric Railway had the unique electrical powered cattle van. No other tramway had such a vehicle. Later the motors were removed and it was used as a trailer.

tramcars from the countryside to the town centre, the empty churns returning by evening trams. There were rumours that some farmers would not use this service because they were afraid that their milk would be butter by the end of the journey, given the rough ride it would be given on the tram. This service was even operated by Leeds tramway, a large city system. The milk churns were collected at Low Green and taken to City Square, where a milkman with his horse and cart met the tram and took the churns for further distribution of the milk.

For one type of tramway farm produce was a staple part of the operations. These were the roadside running Wisbech and Upwell Tramway and the Bessbrook and Newry Tramway. They acted as feeder lines taking locally grown produce to main line railway links. The Bessbrook and Newry tramway used unusual flangeless wagons that were able to be hauled by horses on the ordinary road. This aspect of freight operation is covered in a later chapter.

The Wisbech and Upwell Tramway was run very much on heavy railway operating practices, not surprising as it was built by the Great Eastern Railway, opening in 1883, and eventually became part of British Railways. The region around Wisbech is rich farming land and a major market garden area. The Wisbech and Upwell Tramway provided a link to the main line facilities at Wisbech, while at Upwell there were considerable sidings able to accommodate several hundreds of wagons. When the main crops were harvested some of the trains were exceptionally long for a roadside running tramway. The great advantage of the tramway was that the wagons used were normal railway stock and so would run directly onto the main line railway with no need to transfer the produce. The tramway closed in 1966, but became immortalised in two unusual ways. The unique locomotives used on the line have been used by the late Rev Awdry with Toby the tram engine

29

At the village terminus on the Kinver Light Railway milk churns are very evident with two waiting to be loaded onto the tram and another two to its left.

in his "Thomas the Tank Engine" series, while one of the passenger coaches starred in the comedy film "The Titfield Thunderbolt". The Wantage Tramway offered similar services to the farmers around the Wantage area.

Mention has been made of the small livestock carried by trams, but many systems had authority to carry larger animals such as cows, pigs and sheep. It is assumed that the authorities drafting the legislation envisaged purpose built trailers for such purposes; no passenger would want to share their tram with such animals! As far as can be determined of all the electric

The Kinver Light Railway later had a dedicated milk trailer, the vehicle on the right.

tramways in the British Isles just one made use of these provisions, the Manx Electric Railway. In 1903 the system converted passenger tramcar number 12 to a motor cattle car. There are no records of the usage of the cattle car, but by inference it can be assumed that it was a success because in 1910 two new trailers were built specifically for carrying sheep. In 1912 the cattle car was converted to a trailer by removing its motors. The cattle and sheep trailers lasted until the 1920s when they were broken up, again an assumption has to be made that demand for the services had declined so much they were no longer economic.

Halifax carried milk churns, but only under specific conditions. The rules were "Milk cans will only be carried regularly under special contract and on giving a brass tablet of a design approved by the Tramways General Manager affixed and in no case will they be collected or delivered. Senders and consignees must assist in the loading and unloading of such cans. Milk cans without the aforesaid brass tablet affixed will be carried in accordance with the scale specified in the schedule hereto, or such other scale as shall from time to time be approved by the Council."

In St Helens the tramway was happy to carry milk

On the Castlederg and Victoria Bridge Tramway a train of cattle wagons (the flaps are open) going to market.

churns, though it did stipulate that they must be met at their destination, with a charge of 1d per gallon with empties being carried free. On the Black Country tramways system the Kinver Light Railway ran to the rural village that it was named after. Here trams would pick up milk churns for distribution around the Black Country. Such was the demand that there was a dedicated motorised milk van built from a redundant passenger car in 1918.

The convertable cattle wagons of the Castlederg and Victoria Bridge Tramway in goods mode, with the flaps closed.

31

The Clogher Valley Tramway ran down the main street of Fivemiletown.

In Ireland the Castlederg and Victoria Bridge Tramway, another roadside steam operated line, had convertible cattle wagons. These were standard cattle wagons, but where on the normal type the upper quarter of each side was open for ventilation, the Castlederg wagons had wooden flaps. These were closed when the wagon was not being used for cattle and they became ordinary closed vans. As the majority of cattle movement was on market days, the ability to use the wagons for other produce or goods was useful, though they would need to be well washed out between different uses! Some of these wagons were sold on to the Clogher Valley Tramway, a system some twenty five miles south of the Castlederg and Victoria Bridge Tramway. This was a mixture of street, roadside and private way running in a rural area. It too had much farm traffic. The cattle wagons purchased from the Castlederg and Victoria Bridge Tramway were in fact never used because of buffer height differences (the single central buffer also incorporated the coupling mechanism). However the Clogher Valley Tramway had similar convertible cattle wagons of its own.

The Clogher Valley Tramway had similar convertable cattle vans, here with their flaps closed in goods mode.

Part 4
MINERAL TRAFFIC

Many tramways had works cars that were used to move stones and setts for track laying and maintenance. Some of these cars were designed for this function while other systems used general works vehicles to carry such material. This chapter does not explore this function as it was a normal part of tramway operation. That part of the story is given in the final chapter. This chapter addresses the carrying of bulk minerals that was exceptional, often for use by other organisations or people.

This is possibly the least expected facet of freight operation on British street tramways. In fact there were several tramways that provided a service for mineral traffic, either hauling open wagons or using specially built self propelled wagons. One of the most famous was the only street tramway in Cornwall, the Camborne and Redruth Light Railway. The area was rich in tin and two mines were sunk beside the road between Camborne and Redruth. However, the ore crushing and processing plant was located some distance from the mines and about a mile up an adjoin-

The Camborne and Redruth Tramways had the most extensive mineral service of all the street tramways. Here wagons have been loaded at the mine and are ready to go to the processing plant.

On the Camborne and Redruth Tramways, loading ore at the mine head ready to take it to the processing plant.

ing valley. The mined ore was originally taken by horse and cart, but the building of the tramway offered an easier and cheaper way of moving the heavy ore. So the mine owners arranged with the tramway promoters that the extra lines to the mines and plant were included in the application for the light railway order. Two electric locomotives were purchased in 1903. These were very simple machines with a motorised chassis, open wooden wagon body and a simple sheet metal roof. The ore was carried in open wooden wagons with very small wheels or steel tipper wagons with equally small wheels, with a total of 14 in the fleet. Operation was restricted to between 5am and 7pm, no doubt the residents were thankful of the restrictions as the trains were said to be very noisy. Operation was kept as simple as possible with crude hand operated wood block brakes on the wagons, operated by a man travelling on the last wagon. The passenger tramway closed in 1926, but the mineral traffic continued until 1934.

The Blackpool and Fleetwood Tramroad also ran a mineral service, between Fleetwood and Thornton Gate. The original Act allowing the Blackpool and Fleetwood Tramroad to be built specifically prohibited the carriage of goods weighing over 56 pounds. In 1920 the Blackpool Improvement Act was passed that repealed that section of the previous Act to enable a planned mineral service between Fleetwood and Thornton Gate to commence. The purpose of the changes was not to introduce the service but to deter railway companies from building a rail link to Cleveleys and so remove Blackpool Corporation's monopoly on public transport

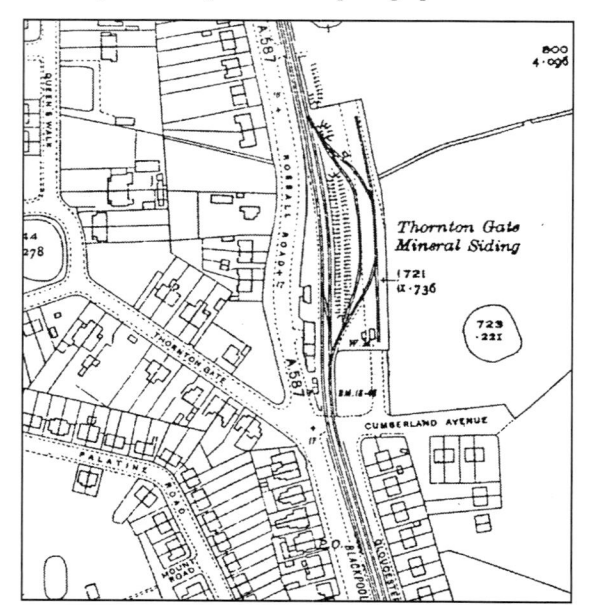

Few homeowners could have had the dubious pleasure of looking out of their front windows to see a line of mineral wagons passing by.

The ramshackle look of the mineral service on the Camborne and Redruth Tramways is well captured in this photograph.

The sidings at Thornton Gate on the Blackpool and Fleetwood Tramroad.

The locomotive shunting coal wagons at Thornton Gate on the Blackpool and Fleetwood Tramroad.

in the area. The Corporation promised to provide the full goods facilities that a railway station would have and they succeeded as the railway companies withdrew their Bill to build the branch line. Having achieved its aim the Corporation was less enthusiastic to start the service. A link between the tramroad and the railway was made at the back of Copse Road tram depot, Fleetwood. Sidings were built at Thornton Gate and the first loads of coal were transported in 1927. The sidings at Thornton Gate were said to have a capacity of 45 wagons, though photos only show a few wagons at any one time. The yard included a coal office and separate dray and rail wagon weighbridges. Only full coal wagons were taken and the promise to provide a full goods service never materialised.

Behind Copse Road depot were the enormous fish dock, curing sheds and the very extensive sidings of the LMS Railway. The tramroad had a rail connection from the side of the depot with the LMS sidings behind the depot building. Steam locomotives from the LMS would shunt wagons full of coal onto the depot yard. Here the Blackpool and Fleetwood small English Electric steeple cab locomotive would haul the wagons to Thornton Gate, where there were tramway sidings. There was no continuous braking, so the wagons were loose coupled with the attendant noise as they rattled to and fro as the locomotive made a slow journey to Thornton Gate. Here the wagons would be unloaded and the coal collected by a local coal merchant for sale around the area. When empty the wagons would be pushed by the electric locomotive back to the depot. The large railway wagons obscured the vision of the driver and so it was the job of the shunter's mate to ride on the first wagon and signal to the driver using green and red flags to indicate when it was clear to proceed. The service always made a loss and the Corporation was ready to abandon it. This opportunity came in 1949. The locomotive was now surplus to requirements and it was offered to the Light Railway Transport League. They declined the offer and so the locomotive was passed to the Corporation works department. Then it was purchased by the National Tramway Museum (now Crich Tramway Village) in 1966 and has been used by the museum as a works vehicle since that date.

The locomotive prepares to push empty wagons back to Fleetwood from Thornton Gate. A pantograph car on passenger service to Blackpool passes by.

Some tramways built powered wagons to carry coal or other mineral traffic, including Huddersfield, Leeds and Southend. Huddersfield had built their tramway to the 4ft 7¾in gauge in anticipation of linking to the

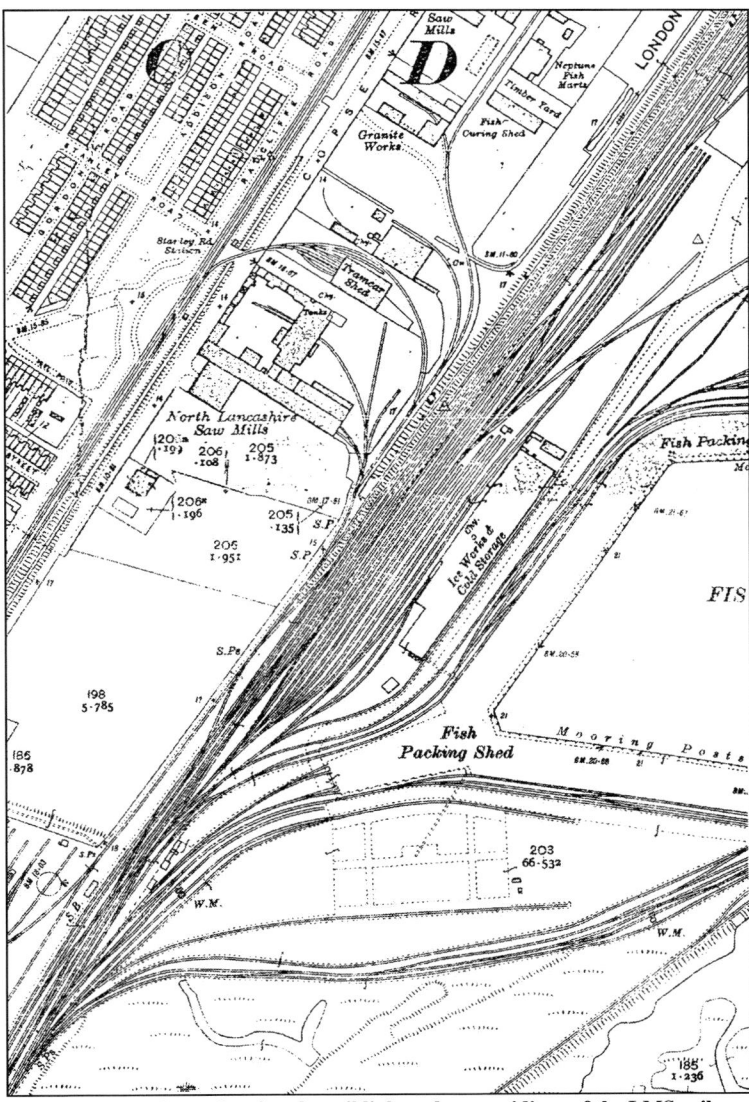

Fleetwood tram depot showing the rail link to the vast sidings of the LMS railway.

35

This photograph clearly shows why the Huddersfield coal tramcar had such a short platform. Even so it only just reaches the coal shoots.

railway and running railway wagons over the tramway. In fact this never came about; however the Corporation gained powers in 1904 to build a spur down Whitestone Lane to the LNWR coal facilities at Hillhouse. This was to provide a coal service to local mills. Two powered coal trucks were purchased from Milnes Voss & Co and originally numbered 71 and 72 (later renumbered 1 and 2). Each could take a 10-ton load, but they had very short platforms for the drivers. The reason for this was that the coal chutes on the LNWR were set at the end of a siding with a brick wall preventing the tracks from being extended. There was very little distance from the coal shoots to the wall so the trams had to have hardly any platform. Local mills that joined the scheme would build a short track in their works that connected with the tramway, usually running in the road alongside the factory. The Corporation then put up the overhead. The service was found to be financially profitable to both the tramway and the mill owners. The service continued until 1934 when the tramway route used by the coal trams closed.

At the beginning of the 20th Century the population of Leeds continued to grow and outstripped the capacity of the water system. In 1906 the Corporation contracted for four new filter beds and a clear water tank to be built near Headingley and the Otley road. The Corporation Water Committee met with the Tramway Committee to agree to the tramway transporting material for the filter beds, collecting materials from the North Eastern Railway Cardigan Road sidings and the construction site. Two special tippler tramcars were built in the tramway workshops. At that date the tramway terminated at Headingley Depot and the filter beds were about half a mile further on. There is no evidence of such an extension being built so it is unlikely that the tramcars were used for this work. In 1909 it was realised that six more filter beds were needed. There were further discussions between the Water and Tramway Committees and as a result a further seven tippler tramcars were built by the tram workshops. This time gravel and sand for the filtering were delivered by river to a wharf near to Swinegate tram depot. The transport of the sand and gravel started in 1910 with the tippler tramcars loading at the wharf and travelling to the filter bed works northwest of Headingley, the route having been extended to West Park in 1908. A temporary tramway connection, complete with overhead, was made between the Otley Road route and the works. The line went between the filter beds allowing the material to be tipped out of the tramcars directly where it was required. It is likely that this service was only required in 1910 and 1911. This left the tramway with a total of nine special tippler tramcars with no work. They became part of the works fleet. They had been made so that the tippler hoppers could be removed allowing the tramcars to be used as flat wagons to carry all kinds of heavy materials.

The situation changed in 1915 when the Leeds Fireclay Company asked the tramway to build a connection between the company's fire clay pits and its works in Upper Wortley. The purpose was to manufacture chemical stoneware, important in the war effort. So the Ministry of Munitions approved the work and the tippler tramcars were usefully employed. Indeed a further three tippler tramcars were built in 1917 to help with the work when an additional line was built to Cardigan Pit. The tramway applied to Parliament for permission to carry heavy goods on the tramway, including coal. To this end a further six tippler tramcars were built in 1921, bringing the total of these special trams to eighteen, by far the largest fleet of specialist mineral tramcars in the whole country. In fact the anticipated coal traffic did not materialise, so the new trams were used to supplement the china clay tram fleet. They continued in service, also being used by the highways and permanent way

Looking at the smoothed pile of coal and the neatly placed shovels, this looks like an official photograph of one of the Huddersfield coal tramcars.

36

Collecting gravel and sand from the river barges for taking to the filter beds being built near Headingley, Leeds.

departments to carry setts for repairing the track. By 1931 the clay reserves in the pits had become exhausted and the company ended its agreement with the tramway. So the tippler tramcars went back to the works department.

In Southend in 1906 there was a proposal to carry coal, not as a revenue earning scheme, but to save money on the existing arrangement of bringing coal by rail. The scheme was to bring coal by sea to the Corporation loading pier (east of the more famous

Leeds had eighteen of these specialised mineral tipper tramcars.

Later the Leeds tippler tramcars were used by the track maintenance gang, here one unloads stone setts for track repairs.

Southend Pier) and then take it by tram to the generating station next to the depot. However, the idea floundered once it was realised that there was not enough room to store the coal at the generating station. The idea was resurrected in 1913 and it was agreed that the loading pier would be refurbished with additional facilities; storage would be made at the tram depot for the coal supplies and three special coal tramcars would be constructed, similar in design to the Leeds tippler trams. All was ready by 1915 and the coal trams carried coal between the loading pier and the depot. The route went from the loading pier left along Southchurch Beach Road right at the Kursaal amusement park into Southchurch Avenue to Southchurch Road and left to the depot. There was no overhead wire on the loading pier, to allow free access for the cranes unloading the coal. So long jumper cables were used to get electricity to the coal trams. Around 1930 the Corporation decided to convert from steam engines to diesel power for generating electricity and the three coal trams fell into disuse, indeed they were dragged off the tracks on the pier.

On the Manx Electric Railway there was a high demand for mineral traffic during the Second World War. It carried rubble spoil from the old mines at Laxey to Ramsey where it was transhipped to lorries and used in the construction of the RAF airfields at Andreas and Jurby. Later the Laxey rubble was taken to Douglas where it was used to widen the promenade.

It is debatable whether the Glyn

The Southend Tramway had three coal tippers to take fuel from the loading pier to the tram generating station.

Another one of the three Southend tipper tramcars.

The Corporation loading pier looking small compared to the main pier behind it. When this photograph was taken the tramway had parked two passenger tramcars on the pier.

Hendre Quarry with Glyn Valley wagons loaded with granite setts.

Valley Tramway is a street tramway or not, but it did run in the road as well as running along the side of the road. While there were significant parts of the route running on reserved track and the operation was far more like a railway than a tramway, this book will treat it as a street tramway. In terms of mineral traffic the Glyn Valley has an interesting history carrying granite, slate and coal. The tramway was built to the unusual gauge of 2ft 4¼in and opened in 1874 with horse power. The first mineral services were the transport of granite, slate and timber down the valley to the Shropshire Union Canal and bringing coal, lime, tiles, bricks and pipes on the return journey. The hauling capacity of the horses was very limited, meaning that trains of wagons needed to be split into a few wagons for uphill sections of the line. It was obvious that the line could be worked more effectively with steam locomotives, so the line was rebuilt for the heavier locomotion. At the same time exchange sidings were built at Chirk to connect with the Great Western Railway, leading to a reduction in the use of the canal. Steam working started in 1888 with the purchase of the Beyer Peacock locomotive "Sir Theodore". Mineral traffic continued to be the major source of income. Granite came from the Hendre Quarry, initially in the form of dressed setts or as chippings. The former were used for the roads of major cities and towns and vast quantities were taken by the tramway in the late Victorian period. As road transport developed in the early part of the 20th Century the demand moved to granite chippings mixed with tar to form tarmacadam. However, the benefit was two edged as road transport began to take the materials from the quarry direct to the roads being laid, without the need to tranship. Slate was quarried from several sites around Glyn Ceirdiog, an industry that started in the 1500s. Slate was the main roofing material in the Victorian age and the tramway was kept busy taking

39

slates to the railway and canal. On the return journey there was a welcome trade in various manufactured goods and also coal. Coal had been mined in Glyn Ceirdiog from the 1600s, but was worked out by the time the tramway opened, so the area had to bring it in from other parts of Wales. Similarly manufactured items, particularly tiles, bricks and earthenware pipes, would be taken up the line. In addition to the freight operation the tramway provided a very useful passenger service to the valley. The tramway continued to operate profitably until the years of the depression in the early 1930s. The drop in demand for slate and granite combined with the increasing competition from road transport meant that the tramway was forced to close in 1935.

When the London County Council began purchasing London's horse tramways and started the conversion to electric operation it was intended that they would generate their own electricity to power the lines. A 3¾ acre site was selected in Greenwich for a new power station and parliamentary authorisation obtained. The power station did not open until 1906, so the LCC had to buy electricity from other producers as the first electrified lines opened. Once on line the Greenwich Power Station supplied the power for all the lines then running. The selected site was alongside the Thames so that coal for the boilers could be delivered by sea-going steamers (the coal came from the Tyneside and Scottish coalfields). A special pier was constructed with cranes that used massive grabs to unload the coal from the ships to coal wagons on a standard gauge industrial tramway.

The tramway had a third rail electrical supply system with two works tramcars. The tramcars hauled the full wagons to the main bunker where they were unloaded by opening hinged floors and dropping the coal into the bunker. The tramcars then returned the empty wagons back to the pier. The trams also hauled ash from the boilers the other way for disposal by ship.

The power station continues to generate power for the London Underground system, having been extended and renovated several times. It supplies extra power for peak time demands and is also an emergency reserve. However, the boilers were converted to oil firing in the 1960s and fuel is now delivered by lorry. The cast iron pier still exists, though it is not used any more. It is not known when the two trams ceased running, but today there is no trace of the rails, or even the decking on the pier.

A train on the Glyn Valley Tramway with a line of slate wagons mixed with passenger carriages.

The Potteries Tramway in Stoke-on-Trent had this tipper tramcar to carry material for permanent way work.

This photograph shows both of the tramcars at the LCC Greenwich Power Station. Sometimes described as locomotives these were definitely tramcars.

A view from the river of the pier and generating station at Greenwich.

Part 5
ROAD-RAIL SERVICES

The first example of road-rail use of street tramways occurred in Liverpool in 1859. Three years earlier W. J. Curtis had patented a 'railway omnibus', a hybrid passenger carriage that could run on the road or, with a flanged wheel device, run on rails. The Liverpool Dock Board had a railway line running along the roadway linking the various docks in the area. Two omnibus companies started running a service on the line in 1859 using the Curtis system of movable flanges. The carriages would be moved off the line to make room for the steam hauled freight services. This is significant as it is a year earlier than the operation considered to be the country's first tramway in Birkenhead that opened a year later in 1860. However, this all concerned passenger transport and this book is focussed on freight.

The Manx Electric Railway was opened in 1893 from Douglas to Groudle Glen, but with aspirations to go further, and eventually the line continued to Ramsey, with the mountain railway to the summit of Snaefell. It is not clear if the idea to carry freight was in the minds of the promoters from the very start, but if not the potential was soon exploited. Soon after the start of operations the system had two open wagons and two closed wagons for goods work, with another open wagon arriving in 1896. In 1899 there was an unusual development. The operators ordered four road-rail wagons from the Bonner Wagon Company, of Toledo, Ohio, USA, though only three were delivered. The vehicles were very similar to typical horse drawn carts of the time, with their own road wheels. The difference came when they were on the track. A special four wheel carrying rail truck was fitted under the carts. So the carts were carried by the trucks along the track. The few surviving photographs show the vehicles being hauled by passenger tram-

At Laxey on the Manx Electric Railway, two Bonner road/rail wagons on their carrier trucks.

cars. The idea was that the carts would be horse drawn along the streets to reach out away from the line, collecting and delivering goods. A contract was soon set up where the carts would collect coal from Ramsey Harbour, go to the line and travel to Ballaglass and then by road to the power station. Then they would go to Doon Quarry to pick up setts to take to the harbour for export. Recent research indicates that the Bonner wagons may not have been used in traffic. It seems very likely that the only journey they made was the one

A special ramp was built to unload the Bonner wagons. They are ready to take the load on the road.

41

would be locked in place for rail travel. Altogether there were 27 such wagons that included open and closed types. When running on the road the wagons were originally horse drawn, but later petrol tractors were used. The system was invented by Henry Varcroft, a director of the Bessbrook Spinning Company. As this arrangement eliminated the need to tranship goods between road and tram vehicles the advantages were considerable. The tramway adopted the arrangement in 1887, just two years after the opening of the line. The road-rail trailers were still in use on the line when it closed in 1948.

Two of the road-rail wagons being hauled by a passenger tram on the Bessbook and Newry Tramway.

for the Press demonstration. It is likely that ordinary wagons were used and the loads transferred to road vehicles. This was a night time operation and residents of Ramsey complained about the noise. This was resolved by transferring to carts in Walpole Drive rather than Ramsey station.

The Bessbrook and Newry Tramway was a mainly rural tramway, but it did have a short section of track that was laid in the roadway. While all the reserved track part of the system had a live third rail providing the power, on the road section there was an overhead wire. The tramcars had bow collectors sprung upwards that contacted the wire to prevent interruption of the power supply. So it can just be allowed to be considered in this book. This is lucky as it had an interesting feature for its goods traffic. The wagons on the tramway had flangeless wheels, to allow use on the public roads. Obviously there was the problem of keeping the flangeless wheels on the tramway rails. This was solved by laying an extra rail, laid outside each running rail and set ⅞ inch below the running rail height. The wagon wheels ran on these extra rails, the running rails acting as a guide to keep the wheels in place and running on top of these extra rails. The wagons had different size wheels at each end. The wheels were loose fitting on the axles to allow the vehicles to take curves easily. The smaller wheels were set on a pivoting axle to enable horses to steer the wagon when being pulled on the roadway. The pivot

The Bessbook and Newry Tramway showing the additional rail to support the road-rail wagons. It is the nearest rail to the camera, fitted alongside the nearer running rail.

A closer look at the road-rail wagons. Both show the smaller front wheels and the open wagon shows clearly the way the smaller wheels pivot for road use.

42

Part 6

OTHER GOODS

Probably the most unusual item of goods to be moved by tramcar was a standard gauge locomotive, made even more odd because the tramway concerned was Cheltenham, a narrow gauge system that did not offer even a parcels service. In 1922 a Manning-Wardle 0-6-0 tank locomotive was taken from St James Station sidings along the tram track to a mineral railway at Sandy Lane. The locomotive had its middle set of wheels removed to allow it to negotiate the sharp tramway bends. Because the tram track was 3ft 6in gauge only the wheels on one side fitted onto a rail. The wheels on the other side were placed on a length of bullhead rail laid on the road surface. A second rail was laid in

Sometimes steam locomotives were seen on the tram tracks of Glasgow.

In the Govan region of Glasgow main line goods wagons ran along the street tramway. Here the electric locomotive owned by the Fairfield shipyard hauls open wagons past a regular passenger tram service.

front of the first and the locomotive dragged by an open top passenger tram. When it was on the second rail the first was moved to the front using a gang of men and horses. In this way the locomotive was dragged slowly through the streets by the tramcar, aided by the horses and men on steep hills. The movement was undertaken on a Sunday when the tramway was normally closed. Taking most of the day the locomotive reached its destination in the evening and it was moved onto the mineral railway tracks.

It must be noted that not all tramways were able to carry goods. The Aberdeen Suburban Tramways had a clause in their Act that stated "The Company shall not carry on the tramways any goods animals or things other than passengers and passengers' luggage and parcels." Paragraphs like this were not entirely unusual as there were all kinds of organisations that could object to a tramway being built and often virtually blackmailed the tramway company into including restrictive clauses in their Act. Most prominent in using this form of persuasion were the railway companies (they feared the competition for their services)

The only known photograph of a Great Orme jockey car. As can be seen the car was dragged off the rails when not required.

and the councils (who often felt they owned the roads and did not want commercial companies interfering with them, unless they got a financial benefit). Of course the latter was not a problem when the council itself promoted the tramway.

Glasgow had a unique freight operation, not run by the Corporation tramway but by two private shipyards and using the street tramway. The story goes back to 1871 when the Vale of Clyde Tramway Act was passed to build a tramway in Govan. Freight traffic was planned from the very beginning, so the unusual gauge of 4ft 7¾in was selected. This slight narrowing of the track would allow main line railway wagons to run on the tramway, where the larger flanges on their wheels would run in the groove of the rails. The aim was to connect the many shipyards and engineering factories along the riverside with the Glasgow and Paisley Joint Railway to give access to the whole country. The Act included authority to connect with the Glasgow Corporation tramway that was being built at the same time. It was necessary that the gauges of the two systems were the same, to allow through running. Glasgow ran some tests and decided to adopt the slightly narrower gauge. This set the gauge for all the tramways in and around Glasgow, despite the fact that the railway wagons only ran on 500 metres of tramway track.

After the tramway opened in 1873, only one of the original four shipyards actually started using the track, Elder's Fairfield works. At this time the freight operation was horse hauled. The first shipment

The Giant's Causeway Tramway with an open wagon in use. The tarpaulin hides the nature of the goods being carried.

Tramcar number 14 used in Gloucester to move goods between the railway and the aircraft works at Brockworth. The framework was built on both sides of the car to carry large items.

44

consisted of four wagons, taking coal, iron sheets and iron plates, each hauled by horses. The great benefit was immediately recognised as the wagon loads arrived at the shipyard without any transhipment. Once unloaded the wagons were collected by a steam locomotive that had been driven to the yard and back to the railway, much against the Act of Parliament. However, in 1876 the tramway obtained authority to use mechanical traction. So steam locomotion was used for passenger operation as well as freight. Electrical power came in 1905 and overhead wire was also laid into the shipyard. The Fairfield yard purchased an electric locomotive and drew power from the tramway overhead by arrangement with the Glasgow tramway. Further west the tram track was used by the yard of Alexander Stephen to take goods traffic to the Shieldhall goods yard. A battery locomotive was used for this operation and so no overhead was erected in the Stephen's yard.

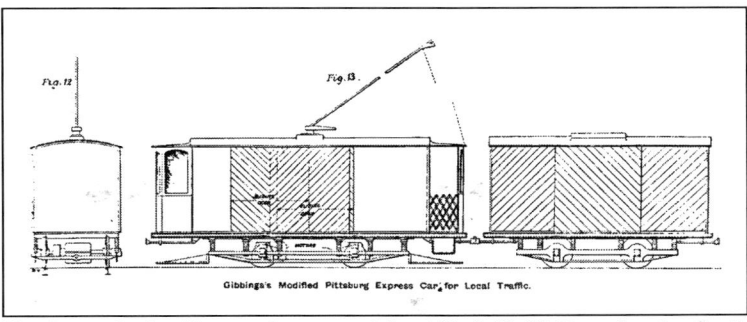

The four wheel rolling stock proposed by Alfred H Gibbings for the South Lancashire freight scheme, as detailed in his paper to the Liverpool Engineering Society in 1902.

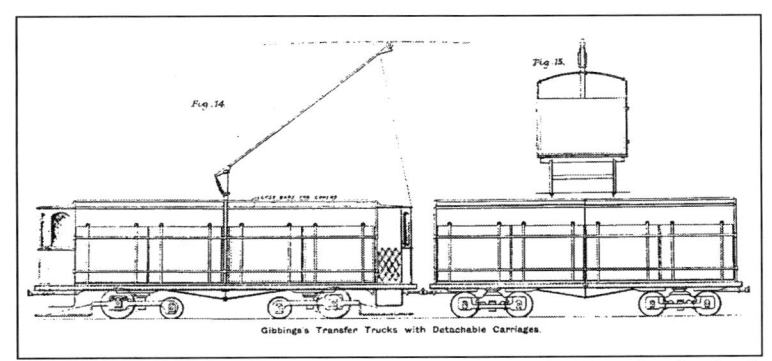

The larger bogie freight stock proposed by Alfred H Gibbings for the South Lancashire freight scheme.

The Alford and Sutton Tramway handled all kinds of freight, mainly in open wagons as shown on this mixed train of goods and passenger vehicles.

45

The Bessbrook and Newry Tramway had more conventional goods vans as well as the road-rail vehicles.

The extensive fleet of horse drawn road vehicles to support the freight operation. Examples of the different loads can be seen in the background.

Surprisingly this use of the tramway continued for eight further years after the rest of the Glasgow system closed in 1960. The Fairfield locomotive was fitted with an additional trolley pole so that it could use both wires of the trolleybus overhead for power (the rails were no longer connected to the power station).

The Great Orme Tramway was another contender for unusual goods operation. When it opened in 1901 it had in addition to the four passenger cars three 'jockey' cars. These were unpowered four wheel goods vehicles. They were attached to the uphill end of the passenger car and pushed up the hill. It was hoped that there would be a profitable trade in goods traffic, but this was not to be so. The regular work consisted of carrying supplies to the summit hotel and coke for the winding house boilers. To reach the summit the 'jockey' car would be hand propelled around the winding house to the upper section of track (in those days there was a loop connection of track between the upper and lower sections). However, there was a far stranger use for the freight cars. They would be used to carry coffins up to a path

A mixed freight train on the Wantage Tramway.

leading to St Tudno's Church and cemetery. Mourners were carried in the usual passenger car while the coffin was taken in the 'jockey' car. Presumably the coffin would then be taken from the tramway to the church on the shoulders of the pall bearers. The tramway had a scale of charges for the coffin and mourners. There is no record of how often this facility was used. There was a road alternative, although the steepness of the road suggests that horse drawn hearses would find the journey difficult if not impossible. So the tramway facility may have been used more often than at first thought. However, all the 'jockey' cars were scrapped by 1911, which suggests that they were not the success the tramway had hoped. It is believed that the jockey cars were also used to transport coal to the central winding house, possibly one jockey car was kept for coal and the other for funerals and clean goods.

Another tramway that had great hopes for a freight service was the first electric tramway in the British Isles. The Giant's Causeway opened in 1883, using hydro-electric power, although steam power was also used. The line served the tourist attraction of the Giant's Causeway, but also provided a welcome rail link between the main line railway at Portrush and the community at Bushmills. It was the latter that the tramway wanted to exploit with the freight service and for this purpose fourteen goods wagons were purchased for the opening of the tramway. However, it seems that the passenger service proved far more popular than the goods service as in 1888 five of the goods vehicles were converted to passenger trailers and another two converted in 1891.The lack of photographs of the wagons in use supports the idea that they were seldom used. But when operated the wagons would be attached to passenger trailers for hauling along the line. Tarpaulins were used to cover the wagon loads, so it is impossible to determine what types of goods were carried.

In 1917 the War Department

Few tramways hauled army gun carriages, but this Bradford tram did exactly that.

Halifax demi-car number 96 was converted to a mobile canteen in 1916 to provide meals to the poorer areas of the town. The limited menu included soup, dumplings and vegetable pie.

Freight on the Dublin and Blessington Tramway, the high side extensions suggest that the truck was used for carrying coke.

47

A brand new Cruden Bay tramcar sparkles in the sun. The open area at the front of the tram was used to carry passengers' luggage and goods for the hotel.

approached the Gloucester City Council regarding the construction of an aerodrome and aircraft works at Brockworth. The Council were asked to build a temporary branch from London Road to the railway goods yard by the station, and extend the tramway from the terminus at Hucclecote to reach the aerodrome. Wartime restrictions meant that there was no rail available. So the track from the little used Westgate Street route was lifted and moved to the aerodrome. The tramway did not have any works cars, apart from a water sprinkler/rail grinder. So passenger tramcar number 14 was converted by removing the glass in the windows and boarding them up. It acquired the nickname "Black Maria" no doubt due to the boarded over windows. It also had large framing fixed to the outside of the lower saloon sides. This allowed oversize items to be fixed to the tram for transport to the aerodrome. There is also a report that it was seen towing a large boiler that was mounted on a temporary bogie.

The most ambitious proposal for freight operation came from the South Lancashire Tramways (SLT). Soon after they had opened the system in 1903 the owners arranged a special trip with six tramcars from Liverpool Pier Head to Bolton Town Hall via Prescott, St Helens, Haydock, Ashton and Atherton, with invitations to civic dignitaries of the councils through which the tramcars were to travel. The trip was a success and during the journey the SLT managers extolled the advantages of operating a through goods service, moving freight to and from the Liverpool docks and the factories around south-east Lancashire. A four wheel tram and trailer design would be used for local

The Cruden Bay Tramway in later years showing the four wheel flat wagon, here used to move ashes and cinders from the hotel boilers.

48

traffic and would have a conventional box van body. There would be special bogie goods trams each with a trailer that could carry 16 tons each. These trams would have detachable tops with a flat open sided chassis. Containers would be loaded onto the trams and trailers. At the factories the containers could be unloaded easily, allowing the tram set to be back in use quickly. However the political difficulties encountered proved too much. First there were objections from the councils to the idea of having goods trams trundling through the streets every five minutes throughout the whole night. Then the tramway systems over which the traffic would travel wanted more tolls for the traffic than the SLT were prepared to pay. Also the difference in wheel profiles for tramways and main line railways

It has not been possible to find a photograph of the freight operation on the Inchture Tramway, so instead this photograph of the horse tramcar that provided the passenger service has been included.

The Manx Electric Railway uses its goods van to advertise its services. A regular passenger service enters Ramsey hauling a goods van.

One of the specialist goods carried by the Manx Electric Railway was laundry. Here the laundry van collects clothes for cleaning. This is at Ramsey.

49

A passenger car hauls two freight wagons over Ballure Viaduct having left Ramsey and is on its way to Douglas. Ramsey Pier is seen in the background.

meant that railway goods wagons could not run on tramway street track and trams could not safely run over railway lines. This problem had been resolved in Glasgow by using a slightly narrower gauge for the tramway. But standard gauge track had already been laid on the existing systems. So any goods traffic would have to be transhipped at each end of the tramway journey. In addition the SLT would have to pay for considerable lengths of track doubling, sidings and goods depots. As a result the scheme was dropped and the only things that the SLT managed to achieve was a limited amount of through passenger running

Manx Electric Railways goods van number 11 at Derby Castle depot.

over St Helens lines and a parcels service.

Whoever drafted the Alford and Sutton Tramway had a very high expectation. The tramway was a steam operated roadside line that had some characteristics of a main line railway, but even so it seems strange that the Act allowed the tramway "for any single piece of machinery or timber or stone or any other single item exceeding 8 tons in weight the tramway could charge such sum as it saw fit". They must have had extremely fit conductors!

Similarly, the rural lines of the Bessbrook and Newry and the Wantage tramway also carried all kinds of other goods traffic. They had a fleet of goods wagons including open trucks and covered vans. In the case of the Bessbrook and Newry they were more conventional than the road-rail wagons previously detailed. The Wantage tramway had a fleet of horse drawn road vehicles for collection and distribution of items in the surrounding area. There were two large canvas covered closed wagons; one had "Wantage Tramway Co Ltd General Hauliers", the other "Wantage Tramway Co Ltd Furniture Removals". In addition there were half a dozen or so two wheel carts for taking small items.

Bradford Tramways also provided a service during the First World War. They fitted a special towing hook and towed gun carriages and ammunition wagons behind the tram. It took them from a Territorial Army Camp in Lister Park across the city to Frizinghall. Here horses took over and completed the journey to Skipton.

The extensive Dublin parcels service has been covered in an earlier chapter. However, it is very much a grey area between other goods and large parcels. So to ensure complete coverage the Dublin system is included in this chapter as well. The tramway carried a whole variety of goods, from barrels of liquids to specialist machinery and everything else between.

During the First World War there were serious food shortages. Horse meat was approved for human consumption in 1916. In Halifax Alderman Spencer was co-opted as the Director of National Kitchens. As part of his programme he suggested that one of the

The goods tramcar and open wagon at the summit on the Snaefell Mountain Railway.

Two Snaefell Mountain Tramway wagons at Bungalow, with two passenger cars in the high distance, at the summit.

51

At the depot on the Snaefell Mountain Tramway showing the water tank and the small four wheel flat wagon that carries it. The wagon is pushed to the summit to provide the Summit Hotel with water.

demi-cars (No 96) be converted into a mobile kitchen. Painted a drab grey and named "National Communal Kitchen" (later changed to "Halifax National Kitchen") the car would go to the poorer areas of the town and provide additional wholesome food to supplement the limited wartime rations. It had electric ovens and hobs to cook the meals, powered from the overhead line through the trolley pole.

The short Cruden Bay Tramway just manages to be included in this book as it had some roadside running, though much was on private way. Built by the Great North of Scotland Railway, the purpose of the Cruden Bay Tramway was to connect the main line at Cruden Bay Station with the Hotel of the same name, also owned by the railway. The tramcars were unusual in having an open end section for carrying passenger's luggage and the Great North of Scotland Railway laundry. The railway company made use of the laundry facilities at the hotel to clean all their linen. So the tramcars were kept busy ferrying large laundry baskets between the railway and the hotel. In addition there was a small four wheel flat wagon that was used to carry ash and cinders from the hotel boilers for disposal.

Also in Scotland the Inchture Tramway had a freight operation. This tramway was built in 1849 to connect the main line of the Dundee and Perth Railway (later becoming part of the Caledonian Railway) from the optimistically named Inchture Station to the village itself, some two miles away. A horse-drawn single deck tramcar carried passengers between the railway and the village. The line also served a brickworks that opened around 1870. Small steam locomotives hauled trains of brick wagons between the factory and the main line. The brickworks closed around 1900 and the sidings were used for an entirely different purpose. Dundee, like all cities of the time, had a problem disposing of the horse manure produced by the motive power of most of the traffic. Indeed one Victorian scientist calculated that by 1950 London would be covered by a six feet deep layer of horse manure. In Dundee the manure generated by the horse trams was transported by train to Inchture and taken on the tramway to the old brickworks siding. Here it would be collected by local farmers for fertilising the land. The tramway had a short life and it closed in 1916. The rails were lifted and shipped to the war in France. However, the ship carrying the rails was sunk in the Channel.

The Manx Electric Railway has made several appearances already and this chapter is no exception. There was a regular contract with one of the island's laundries, where items to be washed and cleaned were moved by the tramway to and from Ramsey. In recent years a motor factor in Douglas has used the tramway to take various motor spares to Ramsey. The procedure was that the vehicle parts would be delivered early in the morning to the Douglas terminus, actually leant against the Inspector's rustic cabin. The first tram of the day would shunt its trailer and the conductor would

In 1982 the Summit Hotel was completely gutted by fire. The tramway was used to carry materials for its rebuilding and the hotel reopened in 1985.

load the goods (tractor tyres and lorry and car exhaust systems have been seen) onto the back of the trailer and the end shutters would be closed to prevent anything from rolling off during the journey. They

Wagons at Snaefell Summit during the rebuilding of the hotel.

The replica works car "Maria" seen here with car 5 in the Snaefell depot.

would be unloaded at Ramsey to await collection. On at least one occasion trailer 56 was used on the first tram. This is the disabled access trailer and it had many of its seats removed for wheelchair use. The tyre and exhaust systems were put on the open area and an obliging passenger kept an eye on them to make sure that they were not lost en route.

The allied Snaefell Mountain Tramway also had a specialist works car and trailers. Named "Maria" the works tram did not have its own bogies, but each winter was fitted with the bogies from car 5. It would take coal to the tramway power station that was located next to the line just below the Bungalow station. Unused for many years the car has subsequently deteriorated badly and is rotting away next to the depot shed. However, in the last few years a replica of the works car has been built and this has its own bogies, using original Snaefell bogies, the passenger cars having been fitted with replacement bogies, using equipment from Aachen, some years ago. It is displayed on special occasions. The tramway also carried goods to the Summit Hotel. There were some four wheel wagons that were pushed to the summit. As well as all kinds of food and sales stock the tramway also had a water tank that could be placed on a flat wagon for carrying water to the summit. These days the goods are taken in a passenger car while the water is still carried by the tank.

Perhaps one of the most common types of goods carried by trams is the child's perambulator (pram) or in these days buggy. When the older systems were operating the prams would be loaded onto the driver's platform, where there was room without interfering with passenger movement. These days, unlike buses, buggies are pushed directly onto the tram and kept in the wheelchair space, without the necessity to take the child out of the buggy and fold it up. This makes the passenger loading of trams much faster than buses.

The Blackpool and Fleetwood Tramroad Company closed their power station at Bispham depot in 1924. During the early part of 1925 the large Lancashire boilers were removed. The company used the tramway to take the boilers to Rigby Road for transporting to Burnley by rail. For the journey a boiler was mounted on two spare bogies and towed on the tram track from Bispham to Rigby Road. For the first part of the journey crossbench car number 139 (a former passenger car relegated to works use) was used until the Blackpool Corporation rails were met at the Gynn. Here Blackpool works car number 2 (an ex Marton Box tramcar) took over the towing, the change being necessary as the wheel profiles of the two systems were at that time significantly different.

More recently there was an unusual use of a tram on a late night service running from Fleetwood to Blackpool. The tramcar stopped on the reserved track at Rossall and the lady driver exited into the dark fields. She re-appeared several minutes later with an armful of heather that was placed in the gangway. She returned to the controls and continued the journey to Rigby Road depot. It is believed that, as well as being a tram driver, she also had a florists shop.

Part 7

INTERNAL FREIGHT

The emphasis has been on revenue-earning freight services; however, many larger tramways had internal freight that needed to be transported around the system. The smaller systems would move equipment and supplies, if they needed to, using their passenger trams. But the amount of internal freight on larger tramways made it economic to have special works cars for this purpose, or to use works cars that would normally be used for specialist purposes, such as water cars or rail grinders.

The material carried by these vehicles varied considerably. Possibly the most common use was to distribute sand between depots. Tramcars used considerable quantities of sand. Each tram had sand hoppers that allowed the driver to spread the sand onto the rails when braking. The sand increased the friction between the wheels and the rail, improving braking and minimising the possibility of getting "flats" on the steel wheels. The sand had to be dried and was usually distributed in sandbags.

In the winter time the tramways wanted to keep their tracks clear of snow and would have either purpose built snow ploughs or snow brooms, or fitted snow ploughs to the front of passenger cars. But some also spread salt over the tracks to melt and clear snow. This was achieved in the simplest of methods. An open wagon full of salt would be pushed in front of a passenger car and maintenance workers would stand on the salt and shovel it over the side onto the road.

In the early days of tramways the roads were often not the metalled surfaces we are used to today, but were packed dirt. In the summer there would be an enormous amount of dust blowing over the

Loaded with bags of sand this Manchester works car is ready to distribute the sand around the system.

London had many stores vans. This was used to carry tickets around the system.

Spreading salt in Manchester with a truck pushed by a passenger tram.

Bradford had a small but interesting fleet of works cars.

55

A very typical water car, used to lay dust on the tram tracks. This example was used in Dublin.

tram tracks. Additionally the natural by-product of the horse traffic, manure, would dry and be broken into a fine powder by other traffic to mix with the other dust.

It surprises some that the dust caused real problems for the tramway. But it would fill in the grooves of the rails and the wheels on the trams would be lifted slightly

The Alford and Sutton Tramway makes use of a covered van to take clinker from the locomotives for disposal elsewhere.

This Metropolitan Electric Tramways car has its own cranes. Useful for lifting heavy objects, like the wheels and axle being loaded in this photograph.

London Transport had two specialist wheel carriers, the sides were planks of wood that could be removed for loading and unloading.

and could lose contact with the rail. This is called being "grounded" and the result is no movement for the tramcar because the electricity is unable to complete its circuit. So there is no power for the motors, it is just like switching the current off, except in one respect. Because the tramcar is no longer earthed it actually becomes the same voltage as the overhead wire. This is no problem to the people on the tramcar as there is no circuit for the electricity to run around. The exception is when someone leaves the tramcar. To prevent any possibility of electrocution it is necessary to jump from the tramcar to the road without holding onto any part of the tramcar. To step off holding the handrail means the circuit is completed and all 400-500 volts is likely to complete its journey through the unfortunate passenger. To minimise the possibility of grounding the tramways would spray water over the road surface, washing away the dust.

On track maintenance duties a Dublin water car hauls a tram of open and flat wagons.

This was undertaken by water cars with large tanks and distribution pipes that would spray water over and around the tracks. In a sense the tramcars were carrying water as freight, albeit delivering it all over the system's routes.

Many of the larger systems such as London County Council and Manchester printed their own tickets. Bulk quantities of tickets then needed distribution around the system. These had to be handled with care as they were the tramway equivalent of cash. In London the LCC had large printing works in Effra Road, Brixton that produced all the tickets for their tramway. These were then distributed to all the LCC depots. The printing works was retained when all the London tramways were amalgamated into London Transport in 1933 and the tickets then had to be taken to the all corners of Greater London, both bus garages as well as tramway depots. In a similar way all the ticket machine maintenance was undertaken by one specialist department and so faulty and mended machines would be taken to and from depot.

A major maintenance item was the replacement of brake blocks. These were made of cast iron and had to be renewed frequently as they wore out. In a similar

In Glasgow a gang works on the permanent way, with setts being carried by works car number 4.

58

The yard of London Transport's Charlton central repair depot was used by both trams and railway wagons. This was possible because the rails had wide and deep grooves to accommodate the larger flanges of the railway rolling stock.

Some works cars were converted from redundant passenger trams, like this one in Sheffield.

vein a heavy user of materials was the track maintenance department. This required the movement of heavy items like lengths of rail, granite setts, overhead traction poles and, in the case of London, the complex conduit. Specialised works cars with flat areas for transporting rails and integral cranes for lifting heavy equipment were used.

It is inevitable that the largest system had the greatest number of internal goods vehicles. When all the different council and company tramways were merged into London Transport in 1933, the capital had around 84 different works cars. Of these, 18 were dedicated stores vans or wagons. So it was not that unusual to see works cars mixing with passenger cars along the streets of London, though the works cars were usually night operators. The fleet was so large it had some rather specialised works tramcars. For example there were two wheel carriers. These were specially strong motorised open wagons that were capable of taking the heavy weight of wheels on their axles and take them for specialist machining. In central London the tramway was equipped for conduit operation, with a slot and electrical supply bars in a channel under the tracks. These were susceptible to corrosion and damage. So salt, brine and grit were never used on these roads. In winter when it snowed the routes were kept open by running tramcars all night. These lighter four wheel vehicles were cheaper to run than the normal bogie passenger tramcars.

Glasgow works car No.28 was a tool van. The smoke comes from the internal stove used to keep the workers warm on cold and wet nights.

Having said that the recently built modern tramways in Britain do not have freight operations, as the last words were being put together on this book two works trams and three works trailers have been purchased by Croydon Tramlink, so possibly some internal freight carrying will be seen on the system.

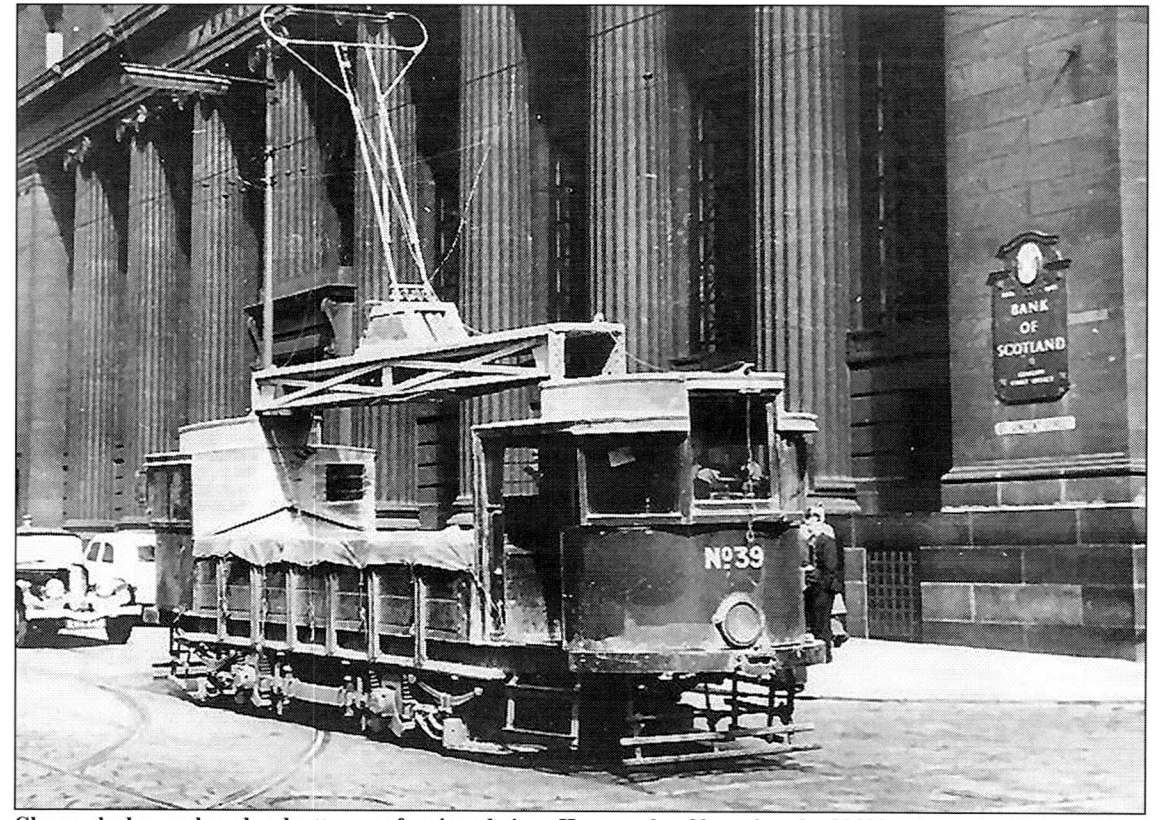

Glasgow had several sand and setts cars of various designs. Here number 39 carries a load hidden from view by tarpaulins.

An earlier view of Glasgow Sand Car No.39 before the centre of the low height cab was raised to make driving more comfortable. This and No.38 had low height cabs to allow them to be driven into the sand drier building.

Glasgow often decorated their trams, but these two must have been the most unusual ever made. A thatched cottage (actually Water Tank car No.13) and a modern villa (car No.50) appeared in 1937 representing civic pride in housing developments, a form of advertising.

Appendix

TRAMWAY SYSTEMS THAT OPERATED A PARCELS SERVICE

Accrington Corporation Steam Tramways Co
Accrington Corporation Tramways
Barnsley & District Electric Traction Co Ltd
Bath Electric Tramways Ltd
Birmingham Corporation Tramways
Birmingham & Midland Tramways Ltd
Blackburn Corporation Tramways
Blackpool and Fleetwood Tramroad Company
Blackpool, St Annes and Lytham Tramways Co
Bradford Corporation Tramways
Brighton Corporation Tramways
Bury Corporation Tramways
Camborne and Redruth Light Railway
Cardiff Corporation Tramways
Castlederg & Victoria Bridge Tramway Co
Cheltenham & District Light Railway
Chesterfield Corporation Tramways
City of Birmingham Tramways Co Ltd
City of Carlisle Electric Tramways Co
Clontarf & Hill of Howth Tramroad Co
Devonport & District Tramways Co
Dublin United Tramways Co
Edinburgh Corporation Tramways
Glasgow Corporation Tramways
Glasgow Tramway and Omnibus Company
Gloucester Corporation Light Railways
Gravesend & Northfleet Electric Tramways Co Ltd
Great Yarmouth Corporation Tramways
Greenock & Port Glasgow Tramways
Halifax Corporation Tramways
Hartlepool Electric Tramways Co Ltd
Huddersfield Corporation Tramways
Ipswich Corporation Tramways
Jarrow & District Electric Traction Co Ltd
Kidderminster & Stourport Electric Tramway Co
Kinver Light Railway
Lanarkshire Light Railway
Leeds Corporation Tramways
Leith Corporation Tramways
Luton Corporation Tramways
Manchester Corporation Tramways
Mansfield & District Light Railway Co
Manx Electric Railway
Merthyr Electric Traction & Lighting Co Ltd
Norwich Electric Tramways Co
Oldham, Ashton & Hyde Electric Tramway Ltd
Peterborough Electric Traction Co Ltd
Pontypridd UDC Tramways
Potteries Electric Traction Co Ltd
Reading Corporation Tramways
Rhonda Tramways Co
South Metropolitan Tramways
South Staffordshire Tramways Co
Stirling and Bridge of Allan Tramway Co Ltd
Sunderland Corporation Tramways
Swansea Improvements & Tramways Co
Wemyss & District Tramways Co Ltd
Wigan Corporation Tramways
Wrexham & District Electric Tramways Co
Yorkshire (Woollen District) Electric Tramways Ltd

TRAMWAY SYSTEMS THAT OPERATED A POSTAL SERVICE

Aberdeen Corporation Tramways
Bexley UDC Tramways
Birkenhead Corporation Tramways
Birmingham Corporation Tramways
Blackpool Corporation Tramways
Blackpool, St Annes and Lytham Tramways Co
Bradford Corporation Tramways
Brighton Corporation Tramways
Camborne & Redruth Light Railway
Chesterfield Corporation Tramways
City of Birmingham Tramways Co Ltd
Cleethorpes Corporation Tramways
Coventry Corporation Tramways

ACKNOWLEDGEMENTS AND SOURCES

As with all my books I owe a massive debt of gratitude to countless people. I have borrowed from the researches of many tramway experts. In addition I have taken every opportunity to bore my friends by constantly asking about goods on tramways and seeking unusual stories. As always they have been exceedingly patient and extremely generous with their time and knowledge. Some have gone even beyond this liberal view and given support that I certainly did not deserve. To those I give my heartfelt thanks, particularly to Alan Kirkman for having an answer to every obscure query and for reading the first draft of the book and for his valuable suggestions to make it more interesting and accurate. I would also like to thank Jim Halsall for information on the Blackburn parcels service and photographs of parcels boys. These are so rare that without Jim's help I would have never been able to find such photographs. I am also indebted to Roger Monk and Geoff Tribe for sending me all kinds of interesting snippets of information that have helped to make the book more entertaining. I also owe many thanks to Adam Gordon, for his endless support and for bringing additional information to light that has helped make the book more interesting and to Trevor Preece for the excellent layout design.

As always I also need to thanks my ever patient family, particularly my wife Elaine who bears with great fortitude my spending hours on a computer writing books; disappearing to visit strange places where there are trams, particularly when we are on holiday; and for giving unparalleled support.

Bibliography

To detail all the sources that I used in compiling this book would result in many more pages than the book itself. So I will just summarise the sources as every book, magazine and article on trams and tramways that I have been able to get hold of.

Croydon Corporation Tramways
Darlington Corporation Light Railways
Dartford UDC Light Railways
Dublin United Tramways Co
Dundee Corporation Tramways
Great Yarmouth Corporation Tramways
Halifax Corporation Tramways
Huddersfield Corporation Tramways
Ilford Corporation Tramways
Keighley Corporation Tramways
Kirkcaldy Corporation Tramways
Leamington & Warwick Electrical Co
Leeds Corporation Tramways
Liverpool Corporation Tramways
Manchester Corporation Tramways
Manx Electric Railway
Middlesbrough Corporation Tramways
Newcastle upon Tyne Corporation Tramways
Northampton Corporation Tramways
Nottingham Corporation Tramways
Nottingham & Derbyshire Tramways Co
Oldham Corporation Tramways
Perth Corporation Tramways
Pontypridd UDC Tramways
Portsmouth Street Tramways Co
Potteries Electric Traction Co Ltd
Rochdale Corporation Tramways
Rotherham Corporation Tramways
Salford Corporation Tramways
Sheffield Corporation Tramways
Snaefell Mountain Railway
Southampton Corporation Tramways
Southport Corporation Tramways
Stockport Corporation Tramways
Sunderland Corporation Tramways
Swansea & Mumbles Railway
Wallasey Corporation Tramways
Walsall Corporation Tramways
West Riding Tramways & Electricity Supply Co Ltd
Wigan Corporation Tramways
Yorkshire (Woollen District) Electric Tramways Ltd

ADAM GORGON

LATEST TITLES

British Tramway Accidents, by F. Wilson
edited by G. Claydon, laminated hardback, 228pp, includes text on over 75 accidents, £35

The Life of Isambard Kingdom Brunel
by his son, reprint of the 1870 edition, softback, 604pp, £20

The Cable System of Tramway Traction
reprint of 1896 publication, 56pp, softback, £10

The Definitive Guide to Trams (including Funiculars) in the British Isles
3rd edition; D. Voice, softback, A5, 248pp, £20

The Development of the Modern Tram
by B. Patton, all colour, 208pp, world-wide coverage, £40

Double-Deck Trams of the World, Beyond the British Isles
B. Patton, A4 softback, 180pp, £18

Double-Deck Trolleybuses of the World, Beyond the British Isles
B. Patton, A4, softback, 96pp, £16

The Douglas Horse Tramway
K. Pearson, softback, 96pp, £14.50

Edinburgh Street Tramways Co. Rules & Regulations
reprint of 1883 publication, softback, 56pp, £8

Edinburgh's Transport, vol. 2, The Corporation Years
919-1975, D. Hunter, 192pp, softback, £20

The Feltham Car
of the Metropolitan Electric and London United Tramways, reprint of 1931 publication, softback, 18pp, £5

TRANSPORT BOOKS

Glasgow Subway Album
 G. Watson, A4 softback, all colour, 64pp, £10

Hospital Tramways and Railways
 second edition, D. Voice, softback, 78pp, £15

How to Go Tram and Tramway Modelling
 third edition, D. Voice, B4, 152pp, completely rewritten, softback, £20

London County Council Tramways
 map and guide to car services, February 1915, reprint, c.12" x 17", folding out into 12 sections, £8

Metropolitan Electric, London United and South Metropolitan Electric Tramways
 routes map and guide, summer 1925, reprint, c.14" x 17", folding out into 15 sections, £8

Modern Tramway, reprint of volumes 1 & 2, 1938-1939
 c.A4 cloth hardback, £38

My 50 Years in Transport
 A.G. Grundy, 54pp, softback, 1997, £10

My Life in Many States and in Foreign Lands
 G.F. Train, reprint of his autobiography, over 350pp, softback, £12

Omnibuses & Cabs, Their Origin and History
 H.C. Moore, hardback reprint with d/w, 282pp, £25

The Overhaul of Tramcars
 reprint of LT publication of 1935, 26pp, softback, £6

Next Stop Seaton! – Golden Jubilee History of Modern Electric Tramways Ltd.
 D. Jay & D. Voice, B5 softback, 136pp, coloured covers, £17

Source books of literature relating to: [all softback]
 Tramways in the East Midlands, 36pp, £4
 Tramways in South-West England, 36pp, £4
 Tramways in Merseyside & Cheshire, 36pp, £4
 Tramways in East Anglia, 28pp, £4
 Tramways in the North East of England, 28pp, £4
 Tramways in N. Lancashire & Cumbria, 39pp, £4
 Tramways in South Central England, 26pp, £4
 Tramways in Scotland, 48pp, £5
 Welsh Tramways, 28pp, £4
 Yorkshire Tramways, 52pp, £5.50

The History and Development of Steam Locomotion on Common Roads
 W. Fletcher, reprint of 1891 edition, softback, 332pp, £18

The History of the Steam Tram
 H. Whitcombe, hardback, over 60pp, £12

A History of the British Steam Tram
 volume 1, D. Gladwin, hardback, coloured covers, 176pp, 312 x 237mm, profusely illustrated, £40

A History of the British Steam Tram
 volume 2, D. Gladwin, hardback, size as above, coloured covers, 256pp, £40

Street Railways, their construction, operation and maintenance
  by C.B. Fairchild, reprint of 1892 publication, 496pp, hardback, profusely illustrated, £40

Toy and Model Trams of the World – Volume 1: Toys, die casts and souvenirs
  G. Kuře and D. Voice, A4 softback, all colour, 128pp, £25

Toy and Model Trams of the World – Volume 2: Plastic, white metal and brass models and kits,
  G. Kuře and D. Voice, A4 softback, all colour, 188pp, £30

George Francis Train's Banquet
  report of 1860 on the opening of the Birkenhead tramway, reprint, softback, 118pp, £10

Trams, Trolleybuses and Buses and the Law before De-regulation
  M. Yelton, B4, softback, 108pp, £15

Tramway Review, reprint of issues 1-16, 1950-1954
  A5 cloth hardback, £23

Tramways and Electric Railways in the Nineteenth Century
  reprint of Electric Railway Number of Cassier's Magazine, 1899, cloth hardback, over 250pp, £23

Tramways – Their Construction & Working
  D. Kinnear Clark, reprint of the 1894 edition, softback, 812pp. £28

Life of Richard Trevithick
  two volumes in one, reprint of 1872 edition, softback, 830pp, £25

The Twilight Years of the Trams in Aberdeen & Dundee
  all colour, A4 softback, introduction and captions by A. Brotchie, 120pp, £25

The Twilight Years of the Edinburgh Tram
  112pp, A4 softback, includes 152 coloured pics, £25

The Twilight Years of the Glasgow Tram
  over 250 coloured views, A4, softback, 144 pp, £25

The Wantage Tramway
  S.H. Pearce Higgins, with Introduction by John Betjeman, hardback reprint with d/w, over 158pp, £28

The Wearing of the Green
  being reminiscences of the Glasgow trams, W. Tollan, softback, 96pp, £12

TERMS

RETAIL UK – for post and packing please add 10% of the value of the order up to £4.90 maximum, orders £50 and over post and packing free. I regret that I am not yet equipped to deal with credit/debit cards.
RETAIL OVERSEAS – postage will be charged at printed paper rate via surface mail, unless otherwise requested. Payment please by sterling cash or cheque, UK sterling postage stamps, or direct bank to bank by arrangement.
SOCIETIES, CHARITIES, etc. relating to tramways, buses and railways – a special 50% discount for any quantity of purchases is given **provided my postal charges are paid.**
WHOLESALE (TRADE) DISCOUNTS FOR MULTIPLE COPIES OF THE SAME TITLE, UK
  post free:
  1-15 copies – 35%; 16-30 copies – 40%; 31-45 copies – 45%; 46 & over – 50%

Apart from being a publisher of tramway titles I buy and sell secondhand literature. I issue lists 4 times a year which contain a selection of books, periodicals, timetables, postcards, tickets and "special/unusual material"; postage is charged at cost and there is no charge for packing. Please send a stamped addressed envelope for the latest list, or if resident abroad, an international reply coupon or UK postage stamps.
I also provide an approval service of black and white plain backed postcards of trams, and hold a stock of over 25,000. The majority of prices vary between £1 & £2, and my only requirements are that customers pay my outward postage and return unwanted cards within a reasonable time. Bus tickets are also sent out on approval, and I have large quantities priced from .05p to £1.

ADAM GORDON, KINTRADWELL FARMHOUSE, BRORA, SUTHERLAND
KW9 6LU
Tel: 01408 622660
E-mail: adam@ahg-books.com
www.ahg-books.com